MW00737162

COUNTERING
BULLYING AND HARASSMENT:

SKILL-BASED LESSONS TO MOVE
FROM BYSTANDER
TO ALLY

Countering Bullying and Harassment:
Skill-Based Lessons to Move from Bystander to Ally

By Jane Harrison

© 2013 Educators for Social Responsibility

esr

Educators for Social Responsibility

23 Garden Street

Cambridge, MA 02138

www.esrnational.org

All rights reserved. With the exception of pages identified as Handouts, no part of this book may be reproduced in any form or by any electronic or mechanical means without permission in writing from the publisher.

Book design by Walter Zekanoski / WZ DESIGN

10 9 8 7 6 5 4 3 2 1
Printed in the United States of America

ISBN 13: 978-0-942349-25-2

COUNTERING
BULLYING AND HARASSMENT:

SKILL-BASED LESSONS TO MOVE
FROM BYSTANDER
TO ALLY

LESSONS FOR SCHOOL...
LESSONS FOR LIFE

FOR GRADES SIX
THROUGH TEN

JANE HARRISON

esr

CONTENTS

FOREWORD & ACKNOWLEDGEMENTS

Countering Bullying and Harassment

The overall approach and specific curricular ideas for building competency and commitment among early adolescents to counter bullying and harassment were developed over the course of many years within ESR. We're grateful for the wisdom and foundational work of Bill Kreidler in *Conflict Resolution in the Middle School;* Carol Miller Lieber, Linda Lantieri, and Tom Roderick in *Conflict Resolution in the High School;* and Jane Harrison and Ken Breeding in *Connected and Respected: Lessons from the Resolving Conflict Creatively Program.*

ESR partnered with Operation Respect in the early 2000s to create the *Don't Laugh at Me* curriculum and to provide training for thousands of people across the country. We thank Peter Yarrow, founder of Operation Respect, and Linda Lantieri, who played the lead role in developing that curriculum, for their creativity and inspiration.

Between 2004 and 2006, ESR developed and piloted the Countering Bullying and Harassment Program. At its core, the program included the creation of peer education programs in middle schools in which a group of students were trained to lead workshops for their peers. Heather Coulehan and Sherrie Gammage were the original authors of the peer education guide used in this program. Heather brought material that she developed working with young people in Anchorage, Alaska. Sherrie served as senior consultant in the pilot project. Together, they forged a powerful approach to putting young people at the center of building a positive peer culture in schools. The guide that they developed is the immediate predecessor to *Countering Bullying and Harassment: Skill Based Lessons to Move from Bystander to Ally.*

ESR developed our peer education guide while collaborating with six middle schools in Massachusetts. These were Andrews Middle School and McGlynn Middle School in Medford, Gibbons Middle School in Westborough, Marlborough Middle School in Marlborough, John F. Kennedy Middle School in Hudson, and the Consentino Middle School in Haverhill. We are grateful for the opportunity to pilot the Countering Bullying and Harassment Program at these schools and thank their school leaders, staff, and students, all of whom provided essential advice, insight, and support for the development of this work.

ESR wishes to acknowledge and thank the following funders whose support contributed to this resource: Lippincott Foundation, The Jessie B. Cox Trust, and The Paul & Edith Babson Foundation.

ESR partnered with Free Spirit Press to co-publish *The Courage to be Yourself* and *A Leader's Guide to the Courage to Be Yourself.* We thank Al Desetta and Sherrie Gammage, the co-authors of these books, for giving voice to students' stories, and for helping adults learn to facilitate student groups that address critical identity issues. We're grateful to Free Spirit Press for permission to use student-written excerpts from *The Courage to Be Yourself* in the lessons in this book.

We thank Carol Miller Lieber for tools and ideas that were drawn from *Making Learning Real: Reaching and Engaging All Learners in Secondary Classrooms* and Carol and co-author Rachel Poliner for ideas incorporated from *The Advisory Guide: Designing and Implementing Effective Advisory Programs in Secondary Schools.*

We appreciate the contributions of the following program consultants, educators, and experts in the field of developing safe, respectful, and welcoming climates that support students to counter bullying and harassment:

Nancy Beardall, originally with the Newton, Massachusetts public schools and now Associate Professor and Program Coordinator in Dance/Movement Therapy, Movement Analysis at Lesley University, supported the development of this curriculum in its initial phases.

ESR staff members who contributed include Lisia Morales, Jeff Perkins, Audra Longert, Denise Wolk, and Jennifer Selfridge.

ESR professional services consultants who helped shape this work include Ken Breeding and Naomi Migliacci. As we moved these lessons into their current form, Carol Miller Lieber, Ken Breeding, M.J. Edwards, and Kerry Lord provided feedback, advice, support, and counsel.

We are deeply grateful to Jane Harrison, the author of *Countering Bullying and Harassment: Skill-Based Lessons to Move from Bystander to Ally.* Jane brought to this project many years of experience working with educators and young people on social and emotional learning, conflict resolution and intercultural relations, and bullying and harassment. She is a former elementary and middle school educator, Resolving Conflict Creatively Program consultant, and *Don't Laugh at Me* trainer. She is also co-author of ESR's two-volume *Connected and Respected: Lessons from the Resolving Conflict Creatively Program.* Jane makes the content of countering bullying and harassment practical and accessible. With elegant and succinct writing, Jane brings her readers a wealth of creative ideas, and she is a pleasure to collaborate with.

Larry Dieringer

Executive Director

Cambridge, Massachusetts 2013

PREFACE

Welcome to this curriculum! It has truly been a labor of love to explore the wonderful materials we at ESR have been using and bring them together into one resource.

As a teacher and trainer of many years, I've seen bullying and harassment close up, and I've watched their terrible effects on both children and adults. There is a reason why adults can remember hurtful words and actions that happened long ago: the pain is sometimes permanent.

I've been so fortunate to work with ESR in different settings all around the world, and I've realized one thing: human beings all have the need to be cherished and appreciated for who they are, no matter how wacky that might be! My own two wacky children had their fair share of pain delivered at the hands of others, and that was sometimes even harder to deal with than my own experiences.

May you use this curriculum to enable young people to cherish and appreciate each other. Being young shouldn't have to be a series of tests with the promise that it will get better. Please find the time to engage students in talking about the things that they say and do to each other that can have such profound effects.

You may find that you, too, are exploring this important topic with a new awareness. How often do we preach that kids should stand up for each other when we, and the other adults in their lives, have such a difficult time doing just that? Being an ally is not such an easy task, but one that is a world-changer.

Yours in Peace,

Jane Harrison

Everyone can remember a time when they experienced bullying. And that's just the problem. The wounds can be felt long after the acts and can have lasting effects on our lives.

The Problem

Fortunately, the days of "kids will be kids" and "what hurts you only makes you stronger" are fading fast. There's too much research that tells us how serious the issue is. Cyber-bullying—the use of technology in bullying—expands the reach and the extent of bullying. Ignoring the issue doesn't make it go away. When adults in the school system ignore bullying or feel that bullying is expected or acceptable, then higher levels of bullying will exist[1].

Bullying has generally been shown to be most prevalent in middle school[2]; however, research has suggested that bullying peaks during school transition (i.e., between elementary and middle school and between middle and high school) as youth are negotiating new peer groups and use bullying as a means to achieve social dominance[3].

According to the National Association of School Psychologists[4], over 160,000 students miss school each day due to fears of being bullied. It stands to reason that bullying detracts from academic achievement, and research supports this negative outcome[5].

This Curriculum

What we can do to address this problem is to provide time for students to discuss bullying and harassment. That's the intent of this curriculum. We know that educators are already overwhelmed with a huge amount of required curricula, and so we've streamlined the lessons that we've found to be effective with students. Each grade level, six through ten, offers six lessons. They are best delivered in sequence and begin with setting guidelines to provide a safe environment for students to discuss these sensitive issues. Without "setting the stage" and creating group guidelines, lessons can lead to unsafe conditions in which students become more vulnerable in front of their peers.

The bonus is that allowing students to talk and share in a classroom also has proven to increase their learning. Students involved in bullying and victimization are less academically engaged[6]; that makes sense with what we know about brain research. A brain that is fearful and on guard is not a learning brain.

From our own experiences with students, we've found that when we are willing to invest the time, we get a lot of "bang for our buck." Students are happier to be in places where they are valued and safe from torment, and adults are happier too, because they don't spend as much time trying to "make" students be nicer to one another and students are actually available to learn, no matter what the subject matter.

Lesson Format

The lessons have been written in a "workshop structure," which encourages a facilitative style of teaching and creates a sense of community structure or ritual whose positive influence extends beyond the scope of the lesson. Each lesson includes:

- **Gathering** (usually 3 – 5 minutes)—An experiential activity or sharing that relates to the main purpose of the lesson and helps students focus on the learning to come. Gatherings are intended to be positive, community-building experiences.
- **Agenda Review** (3 – 4 minutes)—A brief review of what will happen during the lesson that lets students know what to expect. It is most helpful when the Agenda is written on the board or on chart paper.
- **Main Activities** (from 10 – 20 minutes)—Whole class or group activities that provide structured situations that focus on the lesson's subject. Some lessons have more than one activity.
- **Debriefing** (3 – 5 minutes)—A recap that helps students review and internalize what has occurred. It is most important that a Debriefing occur, even if Activities need to be streamlined due to time. Without the opportunity for students to make meaning out of the material, they might not see the relevance of what has been discussed to their own lives.
- **Closing** (2 – 5 minutes)—A quote or exercise to provide closure to the lesson.

Of course, the amount of time devoted to any new learning depends on the facilitator and the students. Often we find that the beginning lessons prove to be much shorter than the time expected, because students are still learning to feel comfortable expressing their opinions. As the comfort level increases, students often want to talk more, and the facilitator can adapt the lessons to this need.

School Climate

These lessons should be one part of creating a positive school climate, the benefits of which have been identified through much research over the last thirty years. A positive on-campus environment reduces the frequency of many problematic behaviors at school, including bullying and harassment. Research has consistently identified an inverse relationship between specific components of positive school climate and bullying among students[7]. A positive climate contributes to more consistent attendance, higher student achievement, and other desirable student outcomes.

Research also documents the importance of school-wide prevention efforts that provide positive behavior support, establish a common set of expectations for positive behavior across all school contexts, and involve all school staff in prevention activities[8].

Administrators, faculty, and staff need to understand and manage student social dynamics, and to handle aggression with clear, consistent consequences. Effective teachers not only promote academic success, they also build relationships, trust, and a sense of community in their classrooms. Additionally, it is crucial that the school seek to create and promote an atmosphere where certain conduct is not tolerated—by students and staff alike. In schools with healthy climates, students know what is appropriate and what is not. Cultivating a positive school climate will not only promote student achievement and success, it will decrease bullying and harassment.

What Students and Teachers Need to Know about Harassment

Many schools, districts, student clubs, and states have adopted guidelines for harassment and bullying. Part of a good prevention program includes providing students with this information. This is best done in the beginning lessons, which deal with identifying bullying and harassment. Students need to know that, should harassment be proved, there are often harsh consequences for the aggressors.

On October 26, 2010, the United States Department of Education published a "Dear Colleague" letter[9] which explains educators' legal obligations to protect students from student-on-student racial and national-origin harassment, sexual and gender-based harassment, and disability harassment. In part, it states, "I am writing to remind you, however, that some student misconduct that falls under a school's anti-bullying policy also may trigger responsibilities under one or more of the federal antidiscrimination laws enforced by the Department's Office for Civil Rights (OCR). As discussed in more detail below, by limiting its response to a specific application of its anti-bullying disciplinary policy, a school may fail to properly consider whether the student misconduct also results in discriminatory harassment."

The statutes that OCR enforces include Title VI of the Civil Rights Act of 1964 (Title VI), which prohibits discrimination on the basis of race, color, or national origin; Title IX of the Education Amendments of 1972 (Title IX), which prohibits discrimination on the basis of gender; Section 504 of the Rehabilitation Act of 1973 (Section 504); and Title II of the Americans with Disabilities Act of 1990 (Title II). Section 504 and Title II prohibit discrimination on the basis of disability. School districts may violate these civil rights statutes and the Department's implementing regulations when peer harassment based on race, color, national origin, sex, or disability is sufficiently serious that it creates a hostile environment and such harassment is encouraged, tolerated, not adequately addressed, or ignored by school employees.

Is Your Classroom Ready for This Curriculum?

This curriculum emphasizes a student-centered approach that follows students' thinking and concerns in ways that build on their own knowledge and connect their own life experiences to what's happening in the larger society.

A curriculum of this type works best in a safe and caring classroom. In a safe classroom all students participate and all students feel that they belong. They know that their individual and cultural differences will be accepted and valued as much as the things that they share in common. Teachers show that everyone counts by balancing the emphasis on individual achievement with a commitment to the well-being of the whole classroom community.

In safe classrooms, students feel comfortable expressing their feelings and concerns. They know that they can make mistakes without being ridiculed, deal with their differences constructively, and disagree respectfully. The lessons in this curriculum work best in a classroom where each student can develop his or her own voice and where listening to peers matters as much as listening to teachers.

Before you begin, it is helpful to know what is occurring in the lives of the students in your classroom. Are students being bullied? Are there some who are targets and some who are perpetrators? Knowing this will help you to facilitate the lessons.

School-wide Commitment

Implementing Bullying Prevention Programs in Schools: A How-To Guide10 by Jones, Doces, Swearer, and Collier provides four important elements that an effective prevention program needs to have:

- A structured curriculum that provides youth with materials over at least several sessions and includes:
  - detailed information on how to implement each lesson
  - lesson materials
  - specific text for presenters
  - procedures for training teachers or other presenters.

One-shot assemblies or pulling a few bits and pieces from a program is not going to make a difference for your youth.

- The program teaches youth new skills. These should be spelled out in the program materials. Research shows that this is critical to helping youth change their behavior. Lecture-only programs do not do this.
- Activities must let youth practice these new skills in active ways. The programs that schools consider should include some combination of classroom discussion periods, engaging and thought-provoking activities, and role-playing.
- For bullying in particular, the program needs to take a whole-school or community approach to prevention. The best programs all offer training for school staff, involvement of parents, and assistance to help the school improve its response to bullying concerns and reports.

Bullying prevention programs will also address the specific needs of students and staff in recognizing, reporting and effectively dealing with bullying incidents. The most effective bullying prevention programs have Social and Emotional Learning components embedded in them. A very strong approach would be to implement both types of programs. Schools can think about SEL programs as a foundation upon which the bullying-specific content should be delivered.

The best SEL programs teach youth the following skills:

- **Self-regulation** (controlling impulses; focusing, sustaining, and shifting attention; listening to and remembering information; empathy training)
- **Perspective-taking** (appreciating similarities and differences; recognizing and identifying the feelings of others; understanding that feelings can change and are complex)
- **Emotion management** (recognizing and identifying one's own feelings; learning strategies for calming down strong emotions; managing stress/anxiety)

- **Problem-solving** (learning a process for solving problems; goal-setting)
- **Communication skills** (being assertive; being respectful; negotiating and compromising)
- **Friendship skills** (cooperation, including others, joining in with others)

Jones, Doces, Swearer, and Collier further state that the best bullying prevention programs should ideally include the above SEL skills and the following:

- Training for all school staff and parents on the "psychology" of bullying
- Training for all school staff and parents on procedures for how to effectively handle bullying reports, including the school's process for and policies around dealing with bullying reports
- Training for teachers on how to deliver the program, including some training around managing relationships and behaviors in the classroom as well as monitoring their own behaviors that are modeled for students
- Training for "Coaches"—people who will work one-on-one with both the students doing the bullying and the students being bullied
- Guidance around establishing policies and procedures, even if it's just a checklist for schools to make sure they are in compliance with district/state/federal laws
- Classroom curricula that:
  - Teach students what bullying is: how to recognize when it's happening to you or someone else
  - Clearly state and reiterate rules, processes, and consequences regarding bullying
  - Teach students assertiveness and communication skills that will help them refuse bullying, whether it is happening to themselves or someone else
  - Teach students skills and strategies for being an effective bystander: supporting the person who was bullied, not joining in, reporting, defusing the situation if possible
  - Teach students skills and the process for reporting bullying, including who to report to
  - All skills must be practiced and reinforced
- Guidance around consequences of bullying:
  - Recommendations for appropriate and graduated consequences, including restorative justice (also sometimes called reparative justice) practice options and mental health interventions, when necessary

Implementation

These lessons have been taught in a variety of settings. Classroom teachers in academic subjects have found that beginning the year with pro-social activities helps to start the year on a positive note. However, there are many other possibilities: advisory, youth leadership programs, new school orientation, freshmen seminars, health education classes, humanities classes, special workshops for students, and out-of-school time youth programs. These lessons can also become a vital part of a peer education program, the potential of which is outlined in an appendix to this curriculum.

Students need a time and a place to discuss the effects of unwanted and unwelcome comments and actions. All students deserve adults in their lives who provide good models, are a listening ear, and who work with them to address the issues.

Bullying and harassment may never totally disappear, but when we intentionally teach how to recognize instances and have ideas on how to deal with them, schools can be safer places to live and learn.

1. Holt, M., Keyes, M., & Koenig, B. (2011). Teachers' attitudes toward bullying. In Espelage, D. L., & Swearer, S. M. (Eds.). *Bullying in North American Schools* (pp. 119-131). New York: Routledge.

2. Nansel, T. R., Overpeck, M., Pilla, R. S., Ruan, W. J., Simons-Morton, B., & Scheidt, P. (2001, April 25). Bullying behaviors among U.S. youth: Prevalence and association with psychosocial adjustment. *Journal of the American Medical Association,* 285, 16.

3. Pellegrini, A. D. & VanRyzin, M., (2011). Part of the problem and part of the solution: The role of peers in bullying, dominance, and victimization during the transition from primary school to secondary school. In Espelage, D. L., & Swearer, S. M. (Eds.). *Bullying in North American Schools* (pp. 119-131). New York: Routledge.

4. Safe Schools and Violence Prevention Office, California Department of Education, (2000). School Attendance Improvement Handbook. Retrieved from http://www.cde.ca.gov/ls/ai/cw/documents/schoolattendance.pdf

5. Glew, G. M., Fan, M. Y., Katon, W., Rivara, F. P., & Kernic, M. A. (2005, January 01). Bullying, psychosocial adjustment, and academic performance in elementary school. *Archives of Pediatrics & Adolescent Medicine,* 159, 11, 1026-31.

6. Nansel, T., Haynie, D., & Simons-Morton, B. (January 01, 2003). The Association of Bullying and Victimization with Middle School Adjustment. *Journal of Applied School Psychology,* 19, 2, 45-61.

7. Gottfredson, G. D., & Gottfredson, D. C. (1985). *Victimization in schools.* New York: Plenum Press.

8. Ross, S. W., & Horner, R. H. (2009). Bully prevention in positive behavior support. *Journal of Applied Behavior Analysis,* 42, 747-759.

9. Ali, R. (2010, October 26). Dear colleague letter. Retrieved from http://www2.ed.gov/about/offices/list/ocr/letters/colleague-201010.html

10. Jones, L., Doces, M., Swearer, S., & Collier, A. (2012, February 23). Implementing bullying prevention programs in schools: A how-to guide. Retrieved from http://www.k12.wa.us/safetycenter/BullyingHarassment/WorkGroup/ImplementingBullyingPrevention-BerkmanCenter.pdf

ASSESSING
STUDENT LEARNING

Before the start of any learning activity, students are likely to ask, "Are we getting a grade for this?" One of the challenges in this work is to develop a variety of meaningful ways to assess students' learning.

Assessing Learning within a Lesson

Through direct questioning, class participation, and discussion, you should be able to get a sense of whether or not your students are grasping the key ideas of each lesson. The Debriefing section of each lesson provides the key concepts of each individual lesson.

Grading Students

Whether you're teaching several lessons, a longer unit, or a quarter or semester course, you might want to consider using a combination of these grading criteria in your class.

_____ % Class Participation

1. Developing Participation Criteria

Taking cues from agreements that you have established in the class with students, you might develop a list of specific behaviors and attitudes that indicate active participation in class. This list might include:

- participating in role plays
- raising thoughtful questions and making comments that help you and the class reach a deeper understanding of an issue or topic of discussion
- taking a leadership role in carrying out an activity
- giving helpful feedback about class activities and experiences
- participating in debriefing and discussion of lesson activities
- taking on various roles and responsibilities in small-group activities
- sharing personal reflections with others in small and larger groups
- helping to set up activities, distribute materials, and clean up
- giving words of encouragement to other students
- laughter and a good sense of humor
- showing appreciation for other students' contributions
- participation in problem solving when issues and concerns arise that affect the group and the class
- willingness to volunteer when help is needed
- ability to focus on a task and complete it
- sharing responsibility within a group, encouraging all students within the group to participate
- taking a risk to try out things that are new and challenging
- friendliness toward other class members
- positive energy when the group needs it
- taking turns recording and documenting small-group work
- ability to work effectively with different students
- showing patience with students who may approach an activity differently

- writing thoughtful reflections when written responses are part of a class activity
- listening to others without interrupting
- respecting other people's privacy and willingness to ask questions or admit confusion
- ability to shift gears from one activity or one way of working to another
- speaking openly and honestly to make others aware of a concern or problem
- being on time for class
- being able to stop and come to closure of an activity when time is up

2. Teacher Feedback and Assessment

You might want to type the above list on a sheet that you can duplicate, so that you have a participation log sheet for each student. Jot down observations of specific behaviors on each student's log sheet that give a snapshot of their participation skills. This snapshot can be a vehicle for giving students personal feedback throughout the class. It can also serve as a starting point for setting goals and checking in on how students are meeting chosen goals, and it can be used when you have conferences with individual students about their participation grades.

3. Student Self-Assessment

Students can also use the criteria list to assess their participation in a number of ways:

- Identify the participation strengths that you already bring to class
- Identify ways to participate that will be challenging for you
- Set goals for what you want to do better
- Reflect back on ways that your participation in class has changed and how those changes have affected how you think and feel about the class and your peers
- Write about one way that you've participated in class that has made a positive difference—something you've done or said that has helped make the class a better learning community for everyone

4. Group Assessment

Keep reviewing and assessing how well the group is keeping agreements you've made together, inviting students to suggest ideas that can help the group with particular agreements that are hard to keep consistently.

Using your agreements as a guide, ask students on an occasional basis to assess what they've done and experienced in class that reflects how they are adhering to these agreements.

_____ *% Skills Assessment*

1. Students can form groups to choose specific skills to demonstrate in a role play or a dramatic skit and videotape it for the class.

2. Students can identify three skills they want to improve and use successfully throughout the course. Students can write about how they have experienced using the skills effectively and also write about situations in which using the skills would have made a positive difference in the outcome of a bullying or harassment situation. The teacher also notes situations in which he or she has observed the student using the skills successfully or situations in which using a particular skill might have made a positive difference.

3. Choose to write about a passage from a novel, short story, or play that illustrates how characters' use of skills in bullying or harassment situations helped them to resolve an issue effectively or how their lack of skills escalated the situation.

4. Choose a video clip from a comedy or drama on TV that illustrates how characters' use of skills in a bullying or harassment situation helped them deal with it successfully or how their lack of skills escalated the situation.

5. Select video clips from film or TV to write about, first analyzing the bullying or harassment situation and then making suggestions about how the parties might deal with the situations successfully.

_____ % Projects (A Sampling of Possible Projects)

1. Students can create a project that illustrates use of skills or lack of skills in dealing with a harassment or bullying situation. For example:
   ◎ Take photographs that show respectful behavior at work in your community or videotape an interview with someone in the community who models anti-bullying behavior.
   ◎ Observe how students bully and harass throughout the day, in classes, in public spaces, etc.
   ◎ Write a story, script, or case study that shows an example of someone dealing in a positive way with an incident of bullying and harassment.
   ◎ Create a public service announcement, advertisement, or video that communicates a message to young people that being an ally to someone being bullied or harassed is a cool thing to do.
   ◎ Design an "Anti-Bullying Tool Kit" that includes the tools and skills your group thinks people need to deal with these issues. Try to use objects to represent the tools; if you can't locate the actual objects, make pictorial representations.
   ◎ Create a TV ad to sell the "Anti-Bullying Tool Kit." This kit has the tools and skills that help people deal with harassment and bullying. Consider making an infomercial.
   ◎ Design a "Bullying Buster." In your group, identify at least five qualities you think someone needs to confront bullying behavior. Create a poster that illustrates what such a "Bullying Buster" would look like.
   ◎ Write a rap song that describes skills that people need to deal with bullying and harassment and that tries to convince them that being an ally for others is cool. Rehearse and perform your song for the class.

- Draw a cartoon or poster that would raise students' awareness of recognizing and dealing with bullying and harassing behavior.
- Stage photographs with the title, "What's Going on Here?" that show common bullying and harassment between adolescents or between adults and adolescents that could be used for discussion in class.

2. Community Action Research Project: Investigate a community example of bullying and harassment that students are concerned about. Respond to the following:

- What is the problem?
- What is your goal?
- What action do you intend to take to achieve your goal? What specific outcome do you hope for and how soon do you expect to achieve it?
- After you have discussed the issue with key individuals and groups, identify other steps your class can take to achieve your goal.
- Why is this a good idea? Why would people in the community support this outcome?
- What is the root cause of the problem? (Lack of resources; clash of values, beliefs, personalities, etc.)
- Who is presently affected by the problem?
- What evidence proves that the problem exists and that specific groups are affected by it?
- Who else may be affected if the problem is not resolved?
- What key individuals and groups need to be part of the problem-solving process? What key resources does each individual or group have that could help you? What decision-making powers do they have?
- Identify three key people or groups who could help you achieve your goal. List at least one common interest you have with each person or group.
- What steps do you need to take before discussing the problem with key individuals or groups? (e.g., documenting the extent of the problem; developing a survey, proposal, or petition; preparing a presentation; interviewing people who could help you get the facts; publicizing a town meeting; identifying key decision-makers needed to approve the necessary change.)

_____ *% Journal Entries*

You may want students to keep journals throughout the lessons to reflect on their experiences in the class, what they notice as a consequence of being in the class, and how they connect what they are learning in class to their own lives.

_____ *% Final Written Assessment of the Class*

See the following Course Assessment Questionnaire (p. 16).

COURSE ASSESSMENT QUESTIONNAIRE

There are several ways that you can use these assessment questions with students:

- ◉ Choose five to ten of these questions for a written assessment.
- ◉ Give students the whole series of questions and invite students to select five to ten to answer.
- ◉ Select some questions for discussion in small and large groups (you might want to tape-record responses) and select some questions for written reflection.
- ◉ Give students the whole series of questions and select a few that you want all students to answer. Invite students to select a few additional questions that they would like to answer.

1. What are three things you want to remember most from these lessons?

2. What are two of the most important things you've learned in this class?

3. What's a skill you've learned and used that has changed your relationship with someone?

4. Describe what you now know about harassment and bullying that you didn't know before.

5. How has learning about cultural differences changed your ideas and feelings about people who belong to different cultural groups than you?

6. List some of the things you do or say to yourself when deciding to confront a bullying or harassment situation.

7. What responses to bullying and harassment did you use most when you started these lessons? What new ones have you learned to use? Describe how you have used them successfully.

8. Has the meaning of any of these words changed for you during these lessons? How?
   - Respect
   - Teasing
   - Bullying
   - Cliques
   - Harassment
   - Rumors and Gossip
   - Instigator
   - Bystander
   - Homophobia
   - Ally
   - Sexual Harassment
   - Sexism
   - Exclusion
   - Racism

9. Describe one thing you've learned about yourself that surprised you.

10. What new questions do you have about harassment and bullying that you'd like to discuss and think more about?

11. In what ways were these lessons taught differently than other courses? Describe three learning activities that were new for you.

12. What aspect of the lessons, what issue, or what activity in the lessons was most challenging? Was there something in the lessons that was difficult for you to do or hard for you to confront?

13. What two or three activities did you like best? Least? Why?

14. What two or three issues and/or activities do you wish all students in your school could experience? Why would you recommend these issues or activities?

15. In thinking back on these lessons, what images and experiences stand out the most for you? Why?

16. What's one way that learning about handling bullying and harassment might change your relationships with your family, classmates, friends, or employers?

17. Describe a bullying or harassment situation that you handled differently because of something you learned in these lessons.

18. Did you feel safe enough in these lessons to take the risk of being open and honest and sharing your stories with others? Why or why not?

19. If you were to summarize what these lessons were about to another student, what would you say? Use two or three sentences.

20. If you were to give advice to teachers about what's most important to keep in mind about teaching these lessons, what would you say? Use two or three sentences.

21. Do you think these lessons will change the rest of your time in school? How? What might you be more aware of or do differently because you participated in these lessons?

22. What's one attitude or skill you hope students in this class will take with them when they leave?

CASEL SEL
COMPETENCIES

The Collaborative for Academic, Social, and Emotional Learning is an organization whose mission is to enhance children's success in school and life by promoting coordinated, evidence-based social, emotional, and academic learning as an essential part of education from preschool through high school. Housed at the University of Illinois at Chicago, CASEL synthesizes the latest empirical findings and theoretical developments and provides scientific leadership to foster progress in SEL research and practice.

CASEL has identified five central competencies to achieve social and emotional literacy. At the start of each lesson in this text, we have provided correlation to the two or three related CASEL competencies. The following chart describes the SEL skill clusters and composite skills CASEL views as essential.

(SA) Self-awareness

Recognizing one's emotions and values as well as one's strengths and challenges

- Accurately assessing one's feelings, interests, values, and strengths; maintaining a well-grounded sense of self-confidence.
- In middle school, students should be able to analyze factors that trigger their stress reactions.
- Students in high school are expected to analyze how various expressions of emotion affect other people.

(SM) Self-management

Managing emotions and behaviors to achieve one's goals

- Regulating one's emotions to handle stress, control impulses, and persevere in overcoming obstacles; setting and monitoring progress toward personal and academic goals; expressing emotions appropriately
- In middle school, students should be able to set and make a plan to achieve a short-term personal or academic goal.
- High school students should be able to identify strategies to make use of available school and community resources and overcome obstacles in achieving a long-term goal.

(SO) Social awareness

Showing understanding and empathy for others

- Being able to take the perspective of and empathize with others; recognizing and appreciating individual and group similarities and differences; recognizing and using family, school, and community resources
- Those in middle school should be able to predict others' feelings and perspectives in various situations.
- High school students should be able to evaluate their ability to empathize with others.

(RS) Relationship skills

Forming positive relationships, working in teams, dealing effectively with conflict

- ⊚ Establishing and maintaining healthy and rewarding relationships based on cooperation; resisting inappropriate social pressure; preventing, managing, and resolving interpersonal conflict; seeking help when needed
- ⊚ Middle school students are expected to demonstrate cooperation and teamwork to promote group goals.
- ⊚ In high school students are expected to evaluate uses of communication skills with peers, teachers, and family members.

(DM) Responsible decision-making

Making ethical, constructive choices about personal and social behavior

- ⊚ Making decisions based on consideration of ethical standards, safety concerns, appropriate social norms, respect for others, and likely consequences of various actions; applying decision-making skills to academic and social situations; contributing to the well-being of one's school and community
- ⊚ Middle school students should be able to evaluate strategies for resisting peer pressure to engage in unsafe or unethical activities.
- ⊚ High-school students should be able to analyze how their current decision-making affects their college and career prospects.

More about the Collaborative for Academic, Social, and Emotional Learning can be found at http://www.casel.org.

Collaborative for Academic, Social, and Emotional Learning. Skills and competencies. Retrieved from http://casel.org/why-it-matters/what-is-sel/skills-competencies/

COMMON CORE ALIGNMENT

English Language Arts

The lessons in this curriculum are aligned to the English Common Core State Standards for English Language Arts. We offer the following overview for subject-area and interdisciplinary educators who plan to implement these lessons with the goal of Common Core alignment.

ELA Common Core State Standards	Countering Bullying and Harassment Lessons
READING	
The standards establish a "staircase" of increasing complexity in what students must be able to read so that all students are ready for the demands of college- and career-level reading no later than the end of high school. The standards also require the progressive development of reading comprehension so that students advancing through the grades are able to gain more from whatever they read.	The readings in the lessons increase in complexity from grades 6 to 10, and the lessons offer opportunities for discussion and analysis of the texts.
Through reading a diverse array of classic and contemporary literature as well as challenging informational texts in a range of subjects, students are expected to build knowledge, gain insights, explore possibilities, and broaden their perspective.	The readings offered in these lessons provide opportunity for students to engage in analysis of non-fiction texts. For example, see the essays from *The Courage to Be Yourself* featured in each grade level's lesson set.
The standards mandate certain critical types of content for all students, including classic myths and stories from around the world, foundational U.S. documents, seminal works of American literature, and the writings of Shakespeare. The standards appropriately defer the many remaining decisions about what and how to teach to states, districts, and schools.	This flexibility creates opportunities for districts and schools in states that have adopted the Common Core to make decisions to include a wide variety of content that includes the type of reading featured in these lessons.
WRITING	
The ability to write logical arguments based on substantive claims, sound reasoning, and relevant evidence is a cornerstone of the writing standards, with opinion writing—a basic form of argument—extending down into the earliest grades.	Students are asked to write throughout this curriculum, with a particular focus on narrative and opinion writing. These lessons provide substantial, engaging, and thought-provoking material for a variety of forms including journal writing, argument construction, narratives, and persuasive writing. When time permits, teachers may wish to extend the writing prompts embedded in these lessons to expand this aspect of Common Core alignment.

ELA Common Core State Standards	Countering Bullying and Harassment Lessons
SPEAKING AND LISTENING	
The standards require that students gain, evaluate, and present increasingly complex information, ideas, and evidence through listening and speaking as well as through media.	The entire orientation of this curriculum is to foster meaningful conversations in order to answer questions, build understanding, and solve problems. Students are required to hone listening skills and speak about complex, challenging, and relevant content. As with writing, teachers may plan to extend and expand the speaking and listening tasks embedded in these lessons.
An important focus of the speaking and listening standards is academic discussion in one-on-one, small-group, and whole-class settings. Formal presentations are one important way such talk occurs, but so is the more informal discussion that takes place as students collaborate to answer questions, build understanding, and solve problems.	This curriculum requires students to work in varied, flexible groupings to discuss and find solutions to problematic scenarios. Mediated but informal conversation is the backbone of this curriculum. We expect that middle and high school teachers will find a high degree of alignment with their states' standards in this area.
LANGUAGE	
The standards expect that students will grow their vocabularies through a mix of conversations, direct instruction, and reading. The standards will help students determine word meanings, appreciate the nuances of words, and steadily expand their repertoire of words and phrases.	These lessons introduce students to new concepts and language through a variety of modes (reading, writing, speaking, and listening). The pace of the lessons ensures that students have ample opportunity to understand and use key words in the area of conflict resolution so that they are integrated into students' understanding and experience.
The standards help prepare students for real life experience at college and in 21st century careers. The standards recognize that students must be able to use formal English in their writing and speaking but that they must also be able to make informed, skillful choices among the many ways to express themselves through language.	This curriculum helps students learn skillful language choices for civil conversation, a critical life skill.
MEDIA AND TECHNOLOGY	
Just as media and technology are integrated in school and life in the 21st century, skills related to media use (both critical analysis and production of media) are integrated throughout the standards.	This curriculum asks students to be media savvy, aware of the messages they send and receive that allow them to protect themselves and their communities. The lessons devoted to cyber-bullying offer additional focus on media use.

The Common Core State Standards highlights presented here were adapted from "Key Points in English Language Arts," available online at http://www.corestandards.org/about-the-standards/key-points-in-english-language-arts.

LESSON

INTRODUCTION

We suggest that in preparation for teaching these lessons, educators share some version of the following script with students, modified according to professional judgment for each grade level:

During the last few years, bullying and harassment have received a lot of attention, and they are now recognized as serious social problems. Movies are being made about bullying and harassment, and not only school polices but also laws have been implemented to address the serious consequences of treating each other badly.

Over the next few weeks, we will be exploring these issues. We'll learn to recognize bullying and harassment, and discuss ways to deal with issues that we experience in our lives. Make no mistake: this is a serious matter. One just has to watch television or read the newspaper to see the damaging effects of mistreatment by others, as well as the legal ramifications that ensue.

Everyone has the right to be treated with respect, and it is our hope that by discussing these issues together, the climate of our classroom and school will be one where bullying and harassment are recognized and addressed, and our environment welcoming and productive.

~

	Lesson 1	Lesson 2	Lesson 3	Lesson 4	Lesson 5	Lesson 6
6th Grade	A Positive Classroom Environment: Setting the Stage for Learning about Bullying and Harassment	Healthy Friendships	Trouble with Teasing: When Teasing Becomes Taunting	Identifying Bullying and Harassment	Dealing with Bullying and Harassment	Moving from Bystander to Ally
7th Grade	Establishing a Safe, Respectful, and Supportive Environment: Setting the Stage for Learning about Bullying and Harassment	Identifying Harassment and Bullying	Dealing with Rumors	Peer Pressure and Exclusion	Roles and Responses in Bullying and Harassment	From Bystander to Ally
8th Grade	Establishing a Safe, Respectful, and Supportive Environment: Setting the Stage for Learning about Bullying and Harassment	Identifying Harassment and Bullying	The Power of Cliques	Understanding Peer Pressure	Roles and Responses in Bullying and Harassment	Being an Ally
9th Grade	Establishing a Safe, Respectful, and Supportive Classroom: Setting the Stage for Learning about Bullying and Harassment	Identifying Bullying and Harassment	Roles in Bullying and Harassment	Understanding Cliques	Cyber-Bullying	Becoming an Ally
10th Grade	Establishing a Safe, Respectful, and Supportive Environment: Setting the Stage for Learning about Bullying and Harassment	Defining Bullying and Harassment	Roles in Harassment and Bullying	Responding to Bullying and Harassment	Interrupting Prejudice and Verbal Abuse	Becoming an Ally

LESSON GRID

GRADE 6
LESSONS ONE – SIX

A Positive Classroom Environment

Setting the Stage for Learning about Bullying and Harassment

CASEL SEL Competencies

SA Self-Awareness
RS Relationship Skills

■ Agenda

Gathering: *Stand Up If ...*

■ Agenda Review

Activity 1: "A Regular Day" Story

Activity 2: The Positive Classroom

Debriefing

Closing: Easy and Hard

■ Materials

2 pieces of construction paper, at least 8½ x 11 inches

Chart paper

■ Prep

Place the Agenda on the board or on a chart

Cut the construction paper into 2 "gingerbread men" shapes

Gathering: *Stand Up If...*

Ask students to stand if the statement you read is true about them.

Stand Up If ...

- You have pets at home
- You have any siblings
- You like to listen to music
- You are good at video games
- You are a good friend
- You have visited another city
- You have a Facebook account

Add any additional items as long as interest is high.

Agenda Review

Just as our Gathering showed that we have some things in common, we can appreciate the fact that we have now come together as a community of students who are here to learn new things and to work together. Sometimes the groups that we work with work well, and sometimes we don't have a positive experience in a group. Ask students to imagine how they would feel if others had laughed when they stood up during the Gathering. It is often those kinds of experiences that make us hesitant to talk about our ideas and opinions openly.

Explain that, as the Agenda shows, you will be telling them a story about one student's day, and the comments that others will choose to make during that day. The next activity will allow us to make some choices about some Agreements that the class will make in order to provide a supportive environment. We will finish with a Debriefing—a time when we talk about what we've learned together. Then, the Closing will return to some personal things to share about ourselves.

Activity 1: "A Regular Day" Story

1. Ask for volunteers to explain what a put-down or "diss" is and share a few examples. (Put-downs or disrespectful comments are ways we make someone feel bad about himself, either with words—name-calling or teasing—or with actions like excluding someone.)

2. Questions:
    ◉ How do these comments make people feel?
    ◉ If people in our class say these things to one another, how might it affect our class environment?

3. Hold one of the paper cutouts in front of you, and explain that the class is going to hear a story about a regular day in someone's life. Give the character the name of someone not in the class. Ask them to listen carefully to the comments that people choose to make to this character.

4. Tell the following story in your own words, or make up a similar story to tell that reflects comments you might hear in your environment. Whenever a character is told a mean comment, tear off a piece of the cutout.

"A Regular Day"

One morning, Sally didn't get up right away when her mother called her. Finally, her mother came in shouting, "Get up, you lazy thing, or you'll be late for school!" *(Rip)* Sally jumped up and threw on her clothes. When she opened her door, her big sister saw her and said, "What's wrong with you, little baby? Can't you even dress yourself? Your shirt is on inside out!" *(Rip)*

Sally ran downstairs to eat, and her little brother laughed, "Ha! I got here first and ate all of the cereal. Sooree!" *[said sarcastically](Rip)* Sally grabbed a piece of fruit, and hurried to get to the bus. She ran fast and just arrived as the bus door was closing. The driver, opening the door said, "What's wrong with you? I can't be waiting around here all day forever!" *(Rip)* Sally stumbled and fell to one knee as she went down the aisle, and lots of kids laughed at her. *(Rip)*

When Sally got to school, she breathed a sigh of relief. She wasn't tardy, thank goodness. But when the teacher asked for her homework, she groaned, realizing that she'd left it on her desk. When she tried to explain this, the teacher said sarcastically, "Sure, Sally, I'll bet your dog ate it!" *(Rip)* When it came time to read aloud from the textbook, she was so nervous that she made a lot of mistakes. She could hear laughter every time she stumbled over a word. *(Rip)* One student even said, loud enough for the class to hear, "Wow, is she dumb!" *(Rip)*

Sally looked forward to her break time, when she at least could see her friends. The day had to get better! All of her friends were gathered in the hallway, and as she approached, everyone stopped talking. "Hi all!" Sally said, and got some frosty looks, "What's up?" Slowly everyone walked away. *(Rip)* Great, she thought. Now, what? She'd heard that her friend Janice had been telling people about a boy she liked, so she said to another friend, Rose, "What's going on?" Rose turned and said, "You shouldn't have done it!" and stomped away. *(Rip)*

Put-downs or disrespectful comments are ways we make someone feel bad about himself.

5. Ask the following:

⊙ How do you think Sally is feeling right now? Why?

⊙ Does this happen in real life?

⊙ How does it feel when it happens?

⊙ What do you think the opposite of a put-down, or being disrespected, is? (a put-up, being positive, being affirming, etc.)

⊙ Can you give me an example of a positive thing one person can say to another?

6. Retell the story, using the second cutout. This time, pause before the negative remark, and ask for positive comments from volunteers. For each positive comment, add some color, or a star, to the cutout. Allow more than one comment each time, if interest is high. When you get near the end of the story, when Sally approaches her friends, have them turn to her instead of walking away. Ask what someone could say to clarify a misunderstanding about a rumor. Perhaps the friend could ask Sally if she actually said or did something that was offensive.

7. At the conclusion of the second reading of the story, ask:

⊙ How do you think Sally is feeling now?

⊙ Why do you think positive statements make us feel better?

⊙ Is there a connection between positive statements and feeling safe to be who you are?

Some teachers have found alternative ways to do this activity. A heart shape can be used (the original activity is called "The Torn Heart"), while some decide to fold the shape each time a negative comment is heard. If that method is chosen, the shape is unfolded in the retelling. Asking students if the shape looks like new when unfolded, which it does not, of course, illustrates the sometimes permanent effects of negative comments.

Activity 2: The Positive Classroom

1. Ask: How would it feel if we decided to try to use positive statements with each other? What kind of Class Agreements can we make to prevent the negative comments, and focus on the positive?

2. Brainstorm a list of possible Agreements. To do this, ask the questions: How would you like to be treated in our classroom? What can we do and say, and others do and say, to make our classroom a safe and positive place to be? Place each contribution on chart paper. Add your own to the list, being careful not to appear lecturing.

3. You might pause after suggestions that are broad in scope, and take a moment to be specific (such as "What makes a good listener?" or "How does someone show 'respect'?"). Many of these items are culturally-linked, and are not universally practiced in the same way. These specifics can be noted on an additional paper, listed on the board as you go, or taught as separate lessons (see Resources Appendix for additional curricula).

We agreed that we would be respectful, and that doesn't feel respectful to me.

4. After everyone has contributed, ask if there are any Agreements that can be combined because they are similar. Make sure that students understand that you are grouping similar ideas, not changing their words.

5. Once each suggestion has been refined into an Agreement, ask students if they can agree to that guideline. Keep in mind that you are working to reach a consensus, so avoid a voting situation.

6. Read each Agreement in its entirety, "We agree to try to be good listeners …" etc.

Debriefing

Ask the following:

- ◉ How do you think these Agreements will help our class?
- ◉ Is there a way we can be gently reminded when we forget to adhere to the Agreements?

Students sometimes come up with harsh punishment because that is what they've heard elsewhere. Point out that it is helpful to practice kind ways to remind others about unfavorable behavior and to say things such as, "I don't like it when you say_____. We agreed that we would be respectful, and that doesn't feel respectful to me."

Closing: Easy and Hard

Ask students to respond to these questions, popcorn style (see the Teaching and Learning Strategies Appendix).

- ◉ What is something that will be easy for you to adhere to in the Agreements we just created?
- ◉ What is something that might be harder?

Healthy Friendships

CASEL SEL Competencies

SA Self-Awareness
SO Social Awareness
RS Relationship Skills

■ Agenda

Gathering: Opinion Poll—
    Friendship on the Line

■ Agenda Review

Activity 1: Good Friendships

Activity 2: Friendship Mural

Debriefing

Closing: Go-Round

■ Materials

Signs labeled "Strongly Agree,"
    "Agree," "Not Sure," "Disagree,"
    and "Strongly Disagree"

Handout—Healthy Friendships

Large sheets of paper and markers
    —one sheet per group

■ Prep

Place the Agenda on the board
    or on a chart

If desired, chart the four
    characteristics of a good
    friendship for Activity 1

Make copies of the handout
    Healthy Friendships—one
    per student

Gathering: Opinion Poll—Friendship on the Line

1. Post five signs around the room labeled "Strongly Agree," "Agree," "Not Sure," "Disagree," and "Strongly Disagree."

2. Explain to the group that you want their opinions on what makes a good friend, so when you read a statement, they should decide whether they strongly agree, agree, disagree, or strongly disagree with the statement. Then students should stand under the sign that reflects their opinion about the statement. Say that you recognize that it's difficult sometimes to not go to where your friends are standing, and instead to decide for yourself.

If they are uncertain about the statement, they should stand under "Not Sure." After each person has moved, ask several people under each sign to explain why they are standing there.

Friendship statements:

- A good friend always agrees with their friend.
- Good friends like to do the same things.
- A good friend never laughs at their friend.
- It's possible to be "friendly" to someone without being their friend.
- Good friends don't argue.
- A good friend never tells their friends' secrets.

Agenda Review

Thank the students for their bravery in choosing where to stand and sharing their opinions. Acknowledge that we all want and need friends. Today we will talk about the meaning of friendship, and how "true friends" not only like us, but support us for who we are, and do not put us in awkward positions by saying things like, "If you like or care about me you will …" They support us and our healthy interests even when these interests are not something they themselves enjoy. Explain that the first Activity will look at the four characteristics of a good friendship, and explore what good friends do and do not say and do for us.

For the second Activity, we'll work in groups to create our visions of a healthy friendship. In the Debriefing, we'll summarize all that we've learned, and then make some promises in the Closing that will make us even better friends.

Activity 1: Good Friendships

1. Explain that good friendships have four characteristics. They are:
   - **Healthy:** Each person supports the other in doing his or her best. You can positively confront a friend. Health is also characterized by honesty and trust, good listening, respect, empathy, shared decision making, and kindness.
   - **Equal:** They are balanced. There are some things you do together and other interests you don't share. Equal friendships allow for freedom, mutual affection, and shared decision-making.
   - **Fun:** There is little stress—friends laugh together and share activities.
   - **Nonviolent:** They are peaceful—emotionally, psychologically, physically, and socially.

2. Distribute the handout Healthy Friendships. Ask students to respond to each of the following prompts:
   - "Friends…"
   - "Friends show us that they care when they…"
   - "Friends don't …"

3. After an appropriate amount of time for students to complete the handout, chart their responses. Tell the group that they may agree or disagree with what is being said, but that the goal is to get as many words as possible for each prompt. Review the student responses by reading aloud the final compilation.

Activity 2: Friendship Mural

1. Divide the class into groups of four or five students (see the Teaching and Learning Strategies Appendix for ideas for random grouping). Explain that they will have 15 minutes to complete a "friendship mural." Using words and/or pictures, the group should portray their thoughts about friendships. The murals will be posted when completed, and each group will have 1 – 2 minutes to explain their mural to the group.

2. Give each group 1 – 2 minutes to explain their mural to the class.

Debriefing

Ask the group the following:

- Why does it sometimes seem harder to speak up to a friend than someone you don't know as well?
- What is the most important thing to you when it comes to friendship?
- What is sometimes difficult about being a good friend?
- What are some responses you've made when a friendship seems to be becoming unhealthy?

Closing: Go-Round

In a go-round, ask each person to answer this question, "How will you be a better friend?" Each person should answer by saying "I WILL …" and then complete the sentence.

Friendships have four characteristics: healthy, equal, fun, and nonviolent.

HANDOUT

Healthy Friendships

Write your responses to each of these prompts:

Friends…

_____

_____

_____

_____

_____

Friends show us that they care when…

_____

_____

_____

_____

_____

Friends don't…

_____

_____

_____

_____

_____

Trouble with Teasing:

When Teasing Becomes Taunting

CASEL SEL Competencies

SO Social Awareness
RS Relationship Skills
RD Responsible Decision-Making

■ Agenda

Gathering: Go-Round

■ Agenda Review

Activity 1: Skit—"Trouble with Teasing"

Activity 2: Role Play— Explaining Different Points of View

Debriefing: When Does Teasing Become Taunting?

Closing: Something to Remember

■ Materials

"Trouble with Teasing" script— two copies

Role-Play cards—one set for each pair of students

■ Prep

Place the Agenda on the board or on a chart

Ask two students to prepare to act out the skit. If the skit doesn't seem applicable, prepare another skit and role-play cards, being sure to portray a conflict about teasing with two equally valid points of view.

Make copies of the Role-Play Cards—one set for each pair of students

Gathering: Go-Round

In a go-round (see the Teaching and Learning Strategies Appendix), ask students to share something they may have in common with many other students. Model by beginning with your own comment, such as, "I like to go to the movies on the weekends."

Agenda Review

As the Gathering showed us, many times we find that we like the same things that other people like. We even sometimes assume that, because we like something so much, others must like it too. Explain that, just as we assume that many people like to do what we do, we often assume that the comments we make will be perceived by others to be the same as we perceive them. For example, if we feel that going to the movies on the weekends is really fun, we almost expect that others like to go to movies also.

Further explain that if we like to tease our friends about the way they do certain things, we assume that our friends will also feel that this teasing is fun. The dilemma is that very often there is a fine line between teasing and taunting, and this lesson will be exploring that concept.

Go on to say, "One person's perception sometimes is not the same as another's. We call that Point of View. If one person sees an event one way, and another sees it differently, a misunderstanding can lead to a great deal of trouble. When teasing feels like taunting, emotions can intensify quickly.

"We'll be watching a skit in which two individuals feel very differently about some remarks. Then, we'll get into pairs and try to see each skit participant's Point of View. Lastly, we'll look at teasing vs. taunting and differentiate between the two, in order to have a better sense of that fine line that is sometimes hard to see."

Activity 1: Skit—"Trouble with Teasing"

1. Have two students perform the "Trouble with Teasing" skit.

2. Questions:
    ⊙ How do you think each person is feeling right now?
    ⊙ Why do you think Student 2 is angry?
    ⊙ Why is Student 1 angry?

Activity 2: Role Play—Explaining Different Points of View

1. Group students into pairs (see the Teaching and Learning Strategies Appendix for suggestions on random pairing).

2. Distribute a set of role-play cards (following this lesson) to each pair so that one receives a card marked Student 1 and one receives a card marked Student 2.

3. Ask students to silently read their role-play cards, and then take turns at explaining their Point of View to the other.

4. After the students have finished, ask:
    ⊙ Why does Student 1 see the remarks he makes as "just teasing"?
    ⊙ How does that differ from Student 2?
    ⊙ Why do you think that Student 2 hasn't said anything up to this point about how he feels about the name-calling?
    ⊙ What's something Student 2 might want to say to Student 1 to let him know how the teasing is perceived?

Debriefing: When Does Teasing Become Taunting?

Ask:
    ⊙ Have you ever had someone get angry with you about a remark you made?
    ⊙ What do you see as the difference between teasing and taunting?

Explain that very often bullying behavior is justified by the comment, "I was just teasing," when in fact the target sees the comments as something quite different. *Teasing* should be fun and lighthearted, with no intention to make the other person feel bad. It is usually done between friends, and is meant to be humorous. Friends stop the teasing when they notice that their comments upset the other person.

Taunting is usually one-sided, and is done to humiliate the other person. The remarks made are often said in a joking manner, but are really cruel and meant to make others laugh at the target. The person doing the bullying will intensify the comments when he or she sees that the target is upset.

Ask students to begin to use these terms to define how comments feel that are made about them. It will raise their awareness to this difference, and allow them to speak up and identify how remarks cross the line from teasing to taunting.

Closing: Something to Remember

Ask students to respond to this question, popcorn-style (see the Teaching and Learning Strategies Appendix): What is something we talked about today that you'd like to remember? Or what is something that you think might be helpful to remember?

Teasing should be fun and lighthearted.

"Trouble with Teasing" Script

Student 1: *(in the cafeteria in front of a long table of friends)*: We're over here! *(waving and trying to get Student 2's attention)*. Hey, Elf Boy! Come sit with us!

Student 2: *(pretending not to hear...)*

Student 1: Elf Boy! *(laughing)* C'mon, we're over here!

Student 2: I'm sitting with someone else.

Student 1: C'mon, we saved you a seat. It's an elf seat! *(friends laughing)*

Student 2: I don't want to sit with you! You're a big jerk!

Student 1: Look who's being a big jerk! I saved you a seat, but forget it. We don't want you to sit here!

Trouble with Teasing Role-Play Cards

Student 1:

Student 1 and Student 2 are good friends. Students 1 calls Student 2 a name in a friendly teasing way, but Student 2 is insulted and the conflict gets worse.

Student 1's Point of View: You think it's cute and funny that Students 2's ears are pointy, and you teasingly kid him about it by calling him "Elf Boy." You're not best friends, but you're good enough friends that you're sure he knows you're kidding. You've been calling him that name for a long time, and it always makes your other friends laugh. You don't know why he's acting touchy about it all of a sudden, and you think he might be putting on a show to get some attention.

Student 2:

Student 1 and Student 2 are good friends. Students 1 calls Student 2 a name in a friendly teasing way, but Student 2 is insulted and the conflict gets worse.

Student 2's Point of View: You've always hated it when Student 1 called you Elf Boy, but you played along with it because you didn't want him to know that it bothered you. But now you've noticed that other friends are starting to call you Elf Boy too. And you can't help but feel that everyone is making fun of you. You can't believe how insulting Student 1 is being and now you're angry and not going to take it anymore!

This role play was adapted from *Don't Laugh at Me: Creating a Ridicule-free Classroom: Teacher's Guide, Grades 6-8* by Peter Yarrow, Mark Weiss, Laura Parker Roerden, and Linda Lantieri (Operation Respect, 2000)

Identifying Bullying and Harassment

CASEL SEL Competencies

SA Self-Awareness
SO Social Awareness
RS Relationship Skills

■ Agenda

Gathering: Go-Round

Agenda Review

Activity 1: Concentric Circles—
Our Experiences

Activity 2: Defining Bullying and
Harassment

Activity 3: Anatomy of a Bully

Debriefing

Closing: New Learning

■ Materials

Chart paper

■ Prep

Place the agenda on the board
or on a chart

Gathering: Go-Round

In a go-round, ask students to respond to the prompt: "Something I'm very proud of is____." Begin the activity with your own contribution.

After everyone has contributed, challenge the students to try to remember another student's response. Allow only one answer per student (for example, "I remember that Jay said he was very proud of his math skills") and see if the class can remember everyone's responses.

Agenda Review

Explain that, in today's Activities, we will be exploring the definition of bullying and harassment. First, we'll talk about our experiences and opinions, and then we'll create a web of words to refine our definition of this issue. Explain that in the Debriefing students will be categorizing the examples into kinds of bullying and harassment, and in the Closing, they will be invited to share their thoughts on how the Activities might have opened them up to some new thoughts and insights.

Activity 1: Concentric Circles—Our Experiences

1. Divide the class into two equal groups. (If you don't have an equal number, you may join one.) One group forms a circle, and then faces outward. The second group forms a second circle around the first one, facing in. Each person in the inner circle faces a partner in the outer circle. (If you don't have enough room to make circles, parallel rows will work. This activity is more fully explained in the Teaching and Learning Strategies Appendix.)

2. Explain that you will be posing a question and then each person will have 2 - 3 minutes to share with their partner; all pairs will speak simultaneously. Identify whether the inside or outside person will speak first. After 2 - 3 minutes, you will signal that the other partner needs to begin to speak. When both partners have answered the first question, ask one of the circles to move two or three spaces to their right. Then pose the second question, and repeat the process. After that question, have the other circle move two places to their right, and so on.

Questions:

- ⊙ Tell about a time when you saw an incident of harassment or bullying at school or in your neighborhood. Who was involved? What happened?

- ⊙ Have you ever heard of anyone being bullied or harassed online or with the use of instant messaging or texting? What happened?

- ⊙ Why do you think people bully or harass others?

3. Bring the class back together and ask for volunteers to answer each of the questions posed.

Activity 2: Defining Bullying and Harassment

1. Write the words "harassment" and "bullying" in the center of the board or on a piece of chart paper. Ask students what words or phrases come to mind when they see these two words. Add their contributed words to the board or chart paper with lines stemming out from the word in the center. You may choose to cluster like responses together. (See the Teaching and Learning Strategies Appendix for a more detailed description of this webbing strategy.)

2. Ask for volunteers to define harassment and bullying based on the ideas generated in the webbing. Write the definitions on the board. One definition might be: Harassment and bullying are any inappropriate, unwanted, or cruel behaviors that make someone feel uncomfortable, threatened, or embarrassed. You might also explain that bullying can be differentiated from harassment. Harassment is linked to aspects of one's identity, e.g., gender, race, sexual orientation, etc.

3. Point out that these are sometimes a single act, but more often are composed of repeated acts performed over time. The target (the person being harassed or bullied) and the aggressor (the person doing it) do not have to agree about what is happening. The aggressor might say, "I was just joking," but if the target feels threatened, then it's harassment or bullying. Aggressors can exert verbal, social, or physical power over a target.

4. Say, "Now that we've created a definition for this kind of behavior, let's brainstorm some of the harassment and bullying you talked about in the first Activity, and categorize them into Verbal, Social, and Physical."

Chart students' responses. Possible responses might include:

Verbal

- ⊙ name-calling
- ⊙ threats
- ⊙ comments on people's appearance
- ⊙ sexual harassment (verbal)

Social

- exclusion
- humiliation
- rumors and gossip
- ignoring people
- mean tricks

Physical

- intimidation
- unwanted touching
- assault
- threatening gestures
- destroying property
- sexual harassment (physical)
- pushing

Activity 3: Anatomy of a Bully

1. Draw an outline of a large gingerbread person on the board, or on chart paper. Ask:
   - What do you think is going on inside of a person who bullies?
   - What do you think they're thinking?
   - How are they acting?
   - What could be happening in their lives?

2. Chart students' responses. Then ask:
   - Is it important to know these things about a bully? Why or why not?
   - What are some strategies for dealing with someone who is a bully?

   Chart these responses on the outside of the gingerbread shape.

3. Explain that in follow-up lessons, students will have the opportunity to generate and practice a wider variety of responses.

Debriefing

Ask the following:
How do you think the information we talked about today will help us? Our class? Our school?

Closing: New Learning

In a go-round, ask each person to share the most valuable or surprising thing they learned about bullying or harassment in this lesson.

"There is no gesture more devastating than the back turning away."

—RACHEL SIMMONS

Dealing with Bullying and Harassment

CASEL SEL Competencies

SM Self-Management
RS Relationship Skills
DM Responsible Decision-Making

■ Agenda

Gathering: "Fashion Un-Conscious" by Nadishia Forbes

Agenda Review

Activity 1: Roles in Harassment and Bullying

Activity 2: Rotation Stations— Questioning Roles

Debriefing

Closing: I Kept Thinking About…

■ Materials

Handout—"Fashion Un-Conscious"

Chart paper—one piece for each of five groups

Markers

Handout—Dealing with Bullying and Harassment

■ Prep

Place the Agenda on the board or on a chart

If desired, chart the Roles in Bullying and Harassment in Activity 1

Write one question from Activity 2 on each of the five pieces of chart paper

Make copies of "Fashion Un-Conscious"—one per student

Make copies of the handout Dealing with Bullying and Harassment—one per student

Gathering: "Fashion Un-Conscious"

1. Read the story "Fashion Un-Conscious" by Nadishia Forbes from *The Courage to Be Yourself: True Stories by Teens About Cliques, Conflicts, and Overcoming Peer Pressure* or have volunteers read a few paragraphs each.

2. Group students into pairs (see the Teaching and Learning Strategies Appendix for suggestions on random pairing). Give pairs 3 minutes to discuss these questions:

   ⊚ Have you ever been teased or harassed about your physical appearance?

   ⊚ What feelings did that trigger and how did it affect your life?

   ⊚ Did you have friends to support you like Nadishia did?

Agenda Review

Bullying and harassment are not new. However, with the advent of technology it has been amplified, and now schools are responding to these issues as never before. Explain that this lesson will be examining the roles people play in harassment and bullying, and begin to explore possible ways to deal with these issues.

Explain that there is no one, perfect way to respond to any harassment or bullying; everyone needs to have a number of choices at their disposal.

The Debriefing will bring all of our brainstorming together, and the Closing will be a time to share a new thought or idea that you've had as a result of our work together.

Activity 1: Roles in Harassment and Bullying

1. Ask the class to brainstorm the different roles that people take in a harassment or bullying situation. List their responses on the board or on chart paper, and then compare them to the ones below:

   ⊚ **Target:** A person or group being harassed or bullied.

   ⊚ **Aggressor:** A person who taunts, threatens, humiliates, victimizes, or physically harms the target. Also known as a bully.

   ⊚ **Instigator:** A person who spreads rumors, gossip, or makes up things to encourage others to harass the target. Instigating can be done verbally, on the Internet, through instant messages, or through graffiti in public places.

- **Bystander:** A person who either witnesses or knows the target is being harassed or bullied and does or says nothing. Bystanders may be adults or even a friend of the target.
- **Ally:** A person who stands up for the target by befriending her or him nonviolently and by challenging the aggressor's attacks.

2. Discuss what it means to be an ally. Emphasize that an ally is peaceful and nonviolent. Point out examples of peaceful and nonviolent struggles, such as the Civil Rights Movement of the 1950s – 1960s, when white, Latino, Native American, and other individuals allied with the African American community as they sought civil rights. What were some of the methods these allies used to help correct a social injustice or wrongdoing? (Mention some examples such as nonviolent marches, boycotts, standing up for victims, and speaking out against Jim Crow laws.)

Ask:
- How do these examples apply to harassment and bullying in schools?

> *"When you start junior high, the pressure to fit in and gain respect is intense."*
>
> —NADISHIA FORBES

Activity 2: Rotation Stations—Questioning Roles

1. Divide the class into five groups (see the Teaching and Learning Strategies Appendix for random grouping ideas, as well as a description of Rotation Stations) and direct each group to stand at one of the areas you have designated. Give each group a piece of chart paper that has one of the following questions written on it:
   - What can *targets* do when they are being harassed or bullied? Where can they get help?
   - What kinds of consequences should there be for *aggressors* at school?
   - Why do people become *instigators*? What can you do to prevent people from instigating conflict and social drama?
   - How can *bystanders* become allies?
   - How can *allies* confront instigators and work to educate the school about bullying and harassment?

2. Allow 2 minutes or so for the group to brainstorm responses to their question and record them on the chart paper. At the end of the time, have all of the groups rotate to another station, leaving their chart paper behind. At their new stations, groups should take another 2 minutes or so to read the question and add their responses to the list started by the previous group. Continue until all of the groups have comments on all of the stations, and have returned to their original questions(s).

3. Ask volunteers from each group to read the question(s) and responses out loud to the class. Discuss the fact that most people play more than one of these roles every day. For example, a person may act as an ally in one circumstance but as an instigator when in a different crowd. (Note: If some of the responses are not nonviolent, remind students of the definition of an ally.)

Debriefing

1. Distribute the handout Dealing with Bullying and Harassment. Discuss after students have read silently, or ask for volunteers to read each section. Ask for any comments. (Note: If students comment that some of the suggestions wouldn't work for them, acknowledge that everyone needs to feel comfortable with the choices they make in dealing with this difficult issue. However, with practice, more choices can become easier to use. Certainly if the environment values dealing with bullying and harassment, and refuses to ignore them, more people will feel comfortable in speaking up.)

2. Students also need to understand that there are legal ramifications to harassment. Should harassment be proved, there are often harsh consequences for the aggressors. The federal government has outlined the legal obligations each school has to protect students from student-on-student racial and national-origin harassment, sexual and gender-based harassment, and disability harassment. Many states have also established additional laws to protect students.

Closing: I Kept Thinking About…

Read the following sentence aloud, filling in the blank with your answer. In a go-round (see the Teaching and Learning Strategies Appendix), ask each group member to do the same.

As we worked together, I kept thinking about…

That experience taught me never to judge people by appearance.

HANDOUT

"Fashion Un-Conscious"

by Nadishia Forbes

Back home in Jamaica, I never really worried about whether my clothes matched. At school, the only thing that used to matter was how clean my uniform was and whether it was ironed. When I went to visit my friends, I would just put on a couple of freshly washed pieces of clothing without even thinking about how they looked.

We were kids—our friendships were not based on appearance. We just liked to run around and have fun. It didn't matter if our braided hair was pointing in all directions and our blouses and skirts had some buttons missing …

I never experienced being judged because of the way I dressed—until I came to the United States. The first time it happened was on my first day of junior high school …

I was a little scared that day, mainly because of the new environment. Walking down the hallway, I felt very self-conscious, so I turned around to get a better look at my classmates.

Two girls were staring at me, whispering and giggling. I stopped and waited for them to pass, but they said to go ahead, so I did. They continued looking at me, but I didn't say anything because I didn't know how to respond.

Even though I didn't hear their conversation, I figured out that it had something to do with the way I was dressed.

They were wearing expensive blue jeans and blouses, the latest name-brand sneakers, and their outfits matched. Plus, they had their hair permed.

I was wearing a pink and black plaid jumper with two straps in front, a blue, red and white striped long-sleeved blouse, thick black stockings, and brown shoes. And I just had big braids in my hair, because my grandmother didn't want me to perm it and that was fine with me.

When I got to my first period class, a couple more of my classmates pointed out my shoes or clothes to their friends and laughed. Some of them even started throwing papers in my direction.

I looked different from everyone else and that was a big problem. When you start junior high, the pressure to fit in and gain respect is intense. The kids who made fun of me were popular—partly because their designer clothes made them seem cool. My clothes made me stand out and gave the others an excuse to pick on me.

I was the perfect target, and it wasn't just because of the way I dressed. I was like a fish outside its water bowl. My classmates saw that I was in a position of weakness and wouldn't stand up for myself. They took advantage of that.

Almost every day, I would be greeted with giggles, pointing, and other demonstrations of their disapproval. For a long time, I didn't have friends to back me up and the teacher did nothing to control the students. Two girls named Luvia and Nefertiti were the main sources of my torment. They would put "kick me" signs on my back, throw papers at me, and make fun of my clothes.

For the first time in my life, I didn't want to go to school. When I got home each day, I would cry and complain to my grandmother about what was happening, but she was too busy to do anything about it.

Sometimes she would say, "Ignore them," or tell me to tell their mothers. Then she would force me to go back to school. She never really understood how hurt and depressed I was.

I would go to school each day with my heart pounding. I hardly paid attention and I never really learned anything. It was hard to concentrate … the other students were very disruptive. Because I was quiet, the teacher always pointed me out as an example to the rest of the class. That made things worse for me.…

I did make one friend that year. Her name was Tina.…We were both from Jamaica … we both had strict families. Tina wore the latest styles of brand-name clothing … but she never judged me.…

Tina would defend me when others were picking on me. She would tell them to leave me alone and always tried to help me out.…

Having Tina as a friend made the days more bearable because I was not entirely alone. But it didn't make much of a difference in terms of how I was treated by the other kids.…

Around the middle of the school term, I started to think that maybe if I dressed like the rest of them, they wouldn't bother me so much.… I was tired of having people treat me like I was beneath them.

One day, I went to school wearing yellow socks and a yellow blouse with a black skirt. Right at the beginning of class, Nefertiti showed Luvia my socks and said, "What are you doing?" with a smirk. It was as if she were saying, "No matter what you do, you won't look as good as we do."

No matter what I did, they wouldn't let up. Luvia, in particular, was always throwing things at me or hitting me. I never started anything with her. She was always coming after me. Then the kids she hung around with would tell her how bad she was.

One day … when she saw me, she hit me. I didn't want to fight, so I started to walk by as I usually did. But for some reason that day, I couldn't take it anymore. I decided it had to stop.

So when I saw Luvia in the cafeteria, I went up to her and slapped her face. The next thing I knew, I was on the floor. Luvia was much bigger than I, so it wasn't much of a surprise when I lost the fight.

That night, I told my father how these two girls had been giving me a hard time.… We went to the counselor's office. She called in Luvia, sat the two of us down, and asked about what was going on between us.

I didn't really hear what the counselor was saying. I was too busy staring at Luvia and wondering what she thought about all this and what the other kids would think when they heard about it.…

After that, Luvia didn't bother me or throw things … but she and her friends still gave me dirty looks.…

In eighth grade, things got better. Everyone started to settle in and feel more comfortable. They let down some of their guard, which made for a less hostile environment.…

I got the chance to make new friends.…and Luvia and Nefertiti weren't in any of my classes anymore, which made everything much easier.…I didn't dread going to school.

That experience taught me never to judge people by appearance. I never tease anyone because of what they wear or how they look. I've also got the best of friends because I didn't pick them based on how they look, but by getting to know them as individuals.

"Fashion Unconscious" by Nadishia Forbes is from *The Courage to Be Yourself: True Stories by Teens About Cliques, Conflicts, and Overcoming Peer Pressure,* used with permission from Free Spirit Publishing

HANDOUT

Dealing with Bullying and Harassment

Here are a few things to consider when you confront or witness teasing, harassment, and bullying:

Ignoring isolated incidents may work, but a consistent problem of harassment will probably continue unless you act to stop it.

Many targets of harassment laugh at the beginning because they are nervous or embarrassed. They may believe or hope that they can just "laugh it off." Often aggressors and bystanders misinterpret the laughter, thinking it means the target doesn't mind.

When you feel uncomfortable or threatened, speak up in a strong, confident, and assertive voice. You have the right not to be harassed! Tell the aggressor firmly, "Don't talk to/touch me like that. I don't like it," "Don't go there. I'm not starting with you—don't start with me," or "That's harassment. If you don't stop, I'll report it."

If you're nervous about nonviolently confronting a person who is an aggressor or an instigator, that's a good indication that it's time to inform adults about the problem. "Walking away" can sometimes be a good option.

Often, the aggressor is angry about something (although being angry does not justify harassing or bullying behavior) that has nothing to do with the target. It may help to ask calmly, "What's up? What are you angry about?" or "Why are you doing that?" Using insults or threats escalates the problem rather than helping to solve it, and can get you in trouble instead of the person who started it.

If you choose to confront someone who is bullying or harassing you, find allies who will speak up, without using threats, to support you. This does not mean finding someone bigger to intimidate the aggressor, because this has the potential to escalate the problem. Many times allies have a different relationship with the aggressor and can intervene successfully.

Without allies, the cycle of harassment and bullying continues unchecked.

Being an ally for others:

If you witness people being harassed or bullied, help them by being a good ally. Speak up without putting anyone down. Try something like, "Let's knock it off," "That's just harsh, there's no reason to go there," "I think that went a bit too far," or "We don't say that kind of stuff here."

You can make similar comments to people who are instigating, saying, "I don't think that's funny" or "That's just a rumor. Drop it."

When speaking to the target, say, "I think they're being cold" or "I think they're looking for trouble. This isn't worth it. Let's get out of here."

It is especially effective if two or more allies speak up, because it helps to prevent the aggressor from turning on a single ally. If you see an ally who is getting picked on, act as an ally for that person and the target by saying something like, "This is getting really old. Can you just drop it already?"

Moving from Bystander to Ally

CASEL SEL Competencies

SM Self-Management
DM Responsible Decision-Making

■ Agenda

Gathering: Pair-Share

Agenda Review

Activity 1: Role Play Preparation

Activity 2: Role Play Presentation

Debriefing

Closing: Yarn Toss

■ Materials

Handout—Guidelines for Allies

Handout—Role-Play Scenarios

Ball of yarn for Closing

■ Prep

Place the Agenda on the board or on a chart

Make copies of the handout Guidelines for Allies, one per student

If desired, chart the role-play guidelines and/or the goals of the role plays outlined in Activity 1, #3.

Make a copy of the handout Role-Play Scenarios, and cut up so that each group receives only one scenario.

Gathering: Pair-Share

1. Group students into pairs (see the Teaching and Learning Strategies Appendix for suggestions on random pairing).

2. Ask the students to take turns summarizing what they have learned in the previous bullying and harassment lessons. Invite them to explain if anything has been a new awareness, something that they hadn't realized before about this complicated subject.

3. Explain that you will signal when 45 seconds is up, and it will be time for the second person to talk.

4. When both participants have spoken, ask for a few volunteers to share what they told their partners.

Agenda Review

Today is an opportunity to put all of our new learning into practice. Our first Activity will be preparing a role play to present to the class, in order to show someone moving from being a bystander to becoming an ally during an incident of harassment or bullying.

During the presentations of those role plays, in Activity 2, the class will identify effective ways to be an ally, in order for us to become more adept in that role.

Explain that the Debriefing will allow the class to create a list of those effective ways, and the Closing will invite us to pledge actions in being an ally.

Activity 1: Role-Play Preparation

1. Distribute copies of the handout Guidelines for Allies. Review the handout, and invite students to use the ideas in their role plays and to add any they think would be effective. Remind students that allies confront the situation nonviolently.

2. Divide the class into five or six groups (see the Teaching and Learning Strategies Appendix for suggestions on random grouping, or if you randomly paired for the Gathering, combine two pairs into a group), and give each small group one of the role play scenarios.

3. Each group should create a brief role play (3 minutes or less) that demonstrates what could happen in this confrontation if an ally helps the target. The point of the role play is to show ways that allies and bystanders can stop harassment or bullying. In their role plays, groups must

- Briefly show what happens during the incident. This should be brief because the emphasis of the role play is on how to help the target, not on the harassment or bullying
- Show the target trying to confront the aggressor or the instigator
- Show the bystander watching the incident
- Show the ally helping in some way

Role Play Guidelines

- You can name the characters and add other details, as long as they do not detract from the main message of how to end the harassment or bullying. Names may not be people you know.
- Do not use bad language or any real physical violence.
- Emphasize how to be a good ally in the role play. Do not emphasize the harassment or bullying. It might be more fun to role play that part, but it is more important that you demonstrate how to be a good ally.
- The role play will be stopped if the guidelines are not followed.

[**Cautionary Note:** *Teachers or other adults should monitor the groups closely to make sure that students who are targets of harassment or bullying in real life are not forced to be targets in the role play. Teachers can assign the roles in each group if this is happening or is in danger of happening.*]

Activity 2: Role Play Presentation

1. Give each group 3 minutes to present their role play to the large group. After each group's presentation, one of the group members should ask the large group these questions:

- What type of harassment or bullying did you see in our role play?
- What ally strategies did we demonstrate?

2. After all six groups have presented their role plays, briefly summarize the ally strategies demonstrated.

Debriefing

Ask:

- What did it feel like to act as an ally in the role plays?
- What did it feel like to be the target?
- How did it feel to have a change of heart as the bystander?

If groups have come up with additional effective comments, add them to the handout.

"Strong people stand up for themselves. Stronger people stand up for others."

Anonymous

Closing: Yarn Toss

Form a large circle. To start the activity, hold a ball of yarn and say: To be a better ally, I will ___, and finish the sentence. Hold on to the end of the yarn, and toss the ball to someone across the circle, and ask that person to complete the same sentence. That person then tosses the ball to someone across the circle, while holding on to their part of the yarn. The next person should complete the sentence and pass the ball, and so on until everyone is holding a strand of yarn.

"All that is necessary for the triumph of evil is that good men do nothing."

Edmund Burke

HANDOUT

Guidelines for Allies

1. If you witness harassment, never enable the aggressor by laughing or stopping to just watch. Help the target by being a good ally. Speak up for him/her without putting anyone down. Try saying something like:
   - "Chill."
   - "Knock it off with the abusive language. No one deserves to hear that."
   - "I don't think that's funny."
   - "That's mean—don't go there."
   - "Where did that come from? We don't say that kind of stuff here."
   - "That's just a rumor. Drop it."
   - "I saw that and it looked like harassment/bullying to me. Lay off."

OTHER THINGS ALLIES COULD SAY …

_____

_____

_____

_____

_____

2. When speaking to the target, say something like:
   - "I think they're being mean."
   - "They're looking for trouble. This isn't worth it. Let's get out of here."
   - "You don't deserve this."

OTHER THINGS ALLIES COULD SAY …

_____

_____

_____

_____

_____

3. It is especially effective if two or more allies speak up, because it helps prevent the harasser or bully from turning on a single ally.

4. Take action. Help the target leave the scene. Go with the target to report the incident or report the incident yourself.

Role Play Scenarios

1. In a classroom, students are taking turns reading aloud from a textbook. The target is making mistakes, and the instigator begins to nudge the aggressor to notice and do something. The aggressor makes nasty comments to the target.

2. All of the students are between classes, on a break, and in the hallways. The aggressor makes fun of the target's personal appearance, to the delight of the instigator, who has encouraged this behavior.

3. During gym class, one student shows that he or she is not skilled at the sport that is being played. The instigator talks to the aggressor a couple of times, pointing at the behavior. The aggressor begins to taunt the target.

4. During the passing period, the aggressor calls the target a name, and uses some threatening language. It becomes clear that there is some history between the two, and that it involves rumors spread by the instigator, who is laughing.

5. It is lunchtime, and the target approaches a lunch table where the instigator and the aggressor are sitting. The target begins to sit down, and the instigator says something to the aggressor, who speaks up about the target not being allowed to sit there.

6. A group of students are in the hallway, all talking about something they've read on Facebook the night before. The target approaches and everyone stops talking. The instigator begins to talk to the others about the postings that concern the target and something he/she is supposed to have done. The aggressor taunts the target about certain behaviors that are outlined in the posting.

GRADE 7
LESSONS ONE – SIX

Establishing a Safe, Respectful, and Supportive Environment

Setting the Stage for Learning about Bullying and Harassment

CASEL SEL Competencies

SA Self-Awareness
RS Relationship Skills

■ Agenda

Gathering: Back-to-Back Sharing

Agenda Review

Activity 1: Safe, Respectful, and Supportive Beings

Activity 2: Group Agreements

Debriefing

Closing: Easy and Hard

■ Materials

Chart paper—one sheet per group of four

Markers—a set per group

■ Prep

Place the Agenda on the board or on a chart

Gathering: Back-to-Back Sharing

Begin by pairing students and asking them to stand back-to-back. (See Teaching and Learning Strategies Appendix for suggestions on random pairing. This is particularly important to do in beginning lessons, as it sets the stage for random pairing each time students participate in a lesson. Once they get used to this method, it becomes easier to get students to speak with others whom they may not know well.) After each question you ask, students will turn to face each other and take turns answering the question. After both students have spoken, they will return to their back-to-back position. After each question, ask for a few volunteers to share their responses with the group.

Before you ask the first question, ask students to think about a time when they felt they were part of a group and felt respected, cared for, and safe being themselves. It may have been a particular class in school, or some other group with whom they worked.

Questions:

⊙ What was it about that experience that made you feel respected, cared for, and safe being yourself?

⊙ How did members of the group treat each other?

⊙ How did people in the group show that they respected each other?

Agenda Review

Explain that, just as they began to explore in the Gathering, today's lesson will give them an opportunity to talk more about being respected, safe, and supported. Say, "As the Agenda shows, we'll be doing an activity called Safe, Respectful, and Supportive Beings. This will help us to create some Agreements about how we'd like to be treated in this classroom, particularly as we begin to talk about the sensitive issues of harassment and bullying.

"The Debriefing will help us to look at our Agreements and think about how to keep them. We'll close with some thoughts about making the Agreements real."

Activity 1: Safe, Respectful, and Supportive Beings

1. Divide students into groups of four (you might randomly assign the pairs used in the Gathering with each other). Each group will create a Safe, Respectful, and Supportive Being on their large sheet of paper.

2. Illustrate a gingerbread person on the board as an example of a shape they might choose to make. Explain that the shape is theirs to decide. They may also choose to name their Being.

3. Ask students to think about what actions, ways of treating each other, and attitudes would make the classroom a place where everyone would feel included and respected.

4. Ask students to write the positive things they brainstorm *inside* the outline of their Being. Some possible things to include might be listening, disagreeing respectfully, etc.

5. *Outside* the outline of the Being, students will place the actions, ways of interacting, and attitudes that they do *not* want as part of the classroom environment, such as name-calling, etc.

6. Allow about 15 minutes for the groups to complete their Beings. It's helpful to notify them when time is half up.

7. Ask each group to share its Being, and post them near each other.

Activity 2: Group Agreements

1. Explain: With the Safe, Supportive, and Respectful Beings that you've created in mind, we're going to build some Agreements that will help us to participate in a positive environment in this classroom.

    Ask:

    ⊚ What words do you notice that we all thought were important and placed in our Beings?

    ⊚ What kinds of Agreements can we make to ensure that these actions and behaviors become a part of our classroom?

2. As students brainstorm suggestions, write them on the board or on chart paper. After everyone has contributed, ask if there are any Agreements that can be combined because they are similar. Make sure that students understand that you are grouping similar ideas, not changing their words.

3. Once each suggestion has been refined into an Agreement, ask students if they can agree to that guideline. Keep in mind that you are working to reach a consensus, so avoid a voting situation.

4. Read each Agreement in its entirety, "We agree to try to be good listeners …" etc. You may also choose to create a classroom Being, writing the guidelines agreed upon inside the Being.

> *"In recognizing the humanity of our fellow beings, we pay ourselves the highest tribute."*
>
> —THURGOOD MARSHALL

Debriefing

Ask the following:

- How do you think these Agreements will help our class?
- Is there a way we can be gently reminded when we forget to adhere to the Agreements?

Students sometimes come up with harsh punishment because that is what they've heard elsewhere. Point out that it is helpful to practice kind ways to remind others about unfavorable behavior and to say things such as, "I don't like it when you say ___. We agreed that we would be respectful, and that doesn't feel respectful to me."

Closing: Easy and Hard

Ask students to respond to these questions, popcorn-style (see the Teaching and Learning Strategies).

- What is something that will be easy for you to adhere to in the Agreements we just created?
- What is something that might be harder?

Identifying Harassment and Bullying

CASEL SEL Competencies

SA Self-Awareness
SO Social Awareness
RS Relationship Skills

■ Agenda

Gathering: A Time I Was New

Agenda Review

Activity 1: Defining Bullying and Harassment

Activity 2: "Afraid to Learn" by Omar Morales

Debriefing

Closing: Go-Round

■ Materials

Handout — "Afraid to Learn"

■ Prep

Place the Agenda on the board or on a chart

Gathering: A Time I Was New

1. Group students into pairs (see the Teaching and Learning Strategies Appendix for suggestions on random pairing).

2. Ask the students to take turns telling their partner about a time they were new in a group. Perhaps it was a time when they changed schools, or perhaps when they joined a group for sports or an activity like scouting. Invite them to give details about how they felt being new, if they had any hesitations about the experience, and how the group treated them as a newcomer.

3. Explain that you will signal when 45 seconds is up, and it will be time for the second person to talk.

4. When both participants have spoken, ask how many had difficult stories to tell. Ask for a few volunteers to explain what those difficulties were, such as feeling excluded or not welcomed.

Agenda Review

Explain that being a new person in a group can sometimes be very difficult and that we can have some bad experiences. Today we will be reading an excerpt from a story written by a boy who was a new student in a school. Before we do, however, we'll spend some time defining the issues the story discusses. Then, we'll hear about Omar Morales' personal experiences with bullying. The Debriefing will allow us to summarize what we've discussed, and then the Closing will give us an opportunity to share a personal connection to what we've learned.

Activity 1: Defining Bullying and Harassment

1. Write the words "harassment" and "bullying" in the center of the board or on a piece of chart paper. Ask students what words or phrases come to mind when they see these two words. Add their contributed words to the board or chart paper with lines stemming out from the word in the center. You may choose to cluster like responses together. (See the Teaching and Learning Strategies Appendix for a more detailed description.)

2. Ask for volunteers to define harassment and bullying based on the ideas generated in the webbing. Write the definitions on the board. One definition might be: Harassment and bullying are any inappropriate, unwanted or cruel behaviors that make someone feel uncomfortable, threatened, or embarrassed. You might also explain that bullying can be differentiated from harassment. Harassment is linked to aspects of one's identity, e.g., gender, race, sexual orientation, etc.

3. Point out that these are sometimes a single act, but more often are composed of repeated acts performed over time. The target (the person being harassed or bullied) and the aggressor (the person doing it) do not have to agree about what is happening. The aggressor might say, "I was just joking," but if the target feels threatened, then it's harassment or bullying. Aggressors can exert verbal, social, or physical power over a target.

4. If the topic does not arise from the discussion, explain to students that "cyberbullying" is a term for acts such as these that occur using the Internet or other digital technologies. In the last few years, it has become as great a concern as traditional bullying, and perhaps greater according to some statistical data. According to the Fall 2010 issue of *Teaching Tolerance*, anywhere from one-third to one-half of youths have been targeted by cyber-bullies. Incidents of online bullying have led to documented incidents of "bullycide," students who take their own lives as a result of the torment from others.

Activity 2: "Afraid to Learn" by Omar Morales

1. Read the excerpt from the story "Afraid to Learn" by Omar Morales (from *The Courage to Be Yourself: True Stories by Teens About Cliques, Conflicts, and Overcoming Peer Pressure*).

2. Write three list headings on the board or on chart paper: Verbal, Social, Physical. Ask the group to name examples of harassment or bullying Omar faced himself or saw happening at his school. As they name the examples, ask them to place them in one of the categories and add them to the appropriate list. Examples from the story include:

Verbal
name-calling
threats

Social
exclusion
humiliation

Physical
intimidation
unwanted touching
assault

> *"I think the reason people in my school were acting this way was because they wanted respect."*
>
> —OMAR MORALES

3. Ask the group to expand the three lists by volunteering kinds of harassment or bullying they have experienced or witnessed at school. Add these to the categories. The lists might expand to the following:

Verbal
sexual harassment (verbal)
comments on people's appearance

Social
rumors and gossip
ignoring people
mean tricks
racism
sexism

Physical
threatening gestures
destroying property
sexual harassment (physical)
pushing

Debriefing

Reviewing the lists, ask group members to identify the four or five most common forms of harassment or bullying that they experience or witness in school. Place an asterisk next to these on the lists.

Closing: Go-Round

Read the following sentence aloud, filling in the blank with your answer. In a go-round (see the Teaching and Learning Strategies Appendix) ask each group member to do the same.

As we worked together, I kept thinking about…

"Afraid to Learn"

by Omar Morales

All my life I've been something of a loner and a sensitive kid. While other kids went out all the time, I was home listening to music, watching television, or just hanging out in front of the building where I live.

But my experience in school made me feel even more alone and made it hard for me to get an education.

Partly, I was just unhappy. But another part of it was that, freshman year, I started getting picked on. In class, one kid would always ask me a question about what the teacher had just said.

I'd answer back, "I don't know."

Then right away he'd start saying, "Damn, you don't know nothing, you're so dumb."

Things like that would happen a lot. Whatever people said would get to me.

For the most part, I thought my school was safe.…But in the middle of freshman year I got a taste of how bad things were going to get.

Before Christmas vacation, I'd had an argument with a kid on the bus. Afterward, I didn't think much about it. But when we returned from break, he attacked me from behind and pummeled me while I was on the ground. I missed two weeks of school because of the bruises inflicted on my face.

After it happened, my mom and I went to the police station and filed a report, but he didn't get arrested. I told the dean of my high school and showed him who did it to me. But he didn't get suspended.

A couple of days after I returned to school, I saw him again on the bus and he was laughing and bragging about beating me up.… I felt humiliated and I felt an anger that I couldn't let go of.

And after that, I just couldn't focus. It's not that I didn't want to learn. I just couldn't get my mind to concentrate.

In my sophomore year, some kids began wearing beads and joining gangs or just forming into groups.… Inside the school, fistfights would sometimes break out. Outside, gangs and smaller groups would walk around looking for someone to rob, intimidate, or beat up. They would look for anyone who seemed weak and they would hurt them for fun. Then they would laugh as they walked away, bragging about what they'd done.…

Every time I was outside the school I had to make sure that I didn't stare at anyone or else he might take it as a challenge. And when I left school I had to make sure that nobody was following me.

This one kid at my school was pressured to rob. Earlier in high school he hadn't been a troublemaker, he was more of a joker. We'd see each other in Resource Room, where we went to get help on our weak subjects.

He would crack jokes about the resource teachers and I would crack up.…

But in sophomore year, some kids from his neighborhood were always trying to convince him to rob somebody after school.

Even though I knew he wasn't the type, twice I saw him hustle some guys for change. He didn't threaten anyone, and it seemed like he didn't

really want to do it. I think he just couldn't say no, especially to his friends.

I think the reason people in my school were acting this way was because they wanted respect. They were probably angry because they didn't get respect anywhere, like in their homes or in their neighborhoods. They probably wanted to show people they were not to be messed with.

But I felt it was wrong to hurt other people for no reason. When I saw kids getting beat up, I sympathized with them because I knew how they felt when they went home, bruised and humiliated....

By the end of my junior year, the safety around the school did improve. Now when I go to school I see police outside a lot more of the time. Things seem safer....

Sometimes I think it would have been better if I had been more aggressive and just knocked someone after he said one word to me. But then I realize that wouldn't have solved anything.

I may have thought I was weak compared to the tough guys, but there was one good thing about being quiet and a loner. I didn't feel pressured to do things I knew were wrong. I didn't have to prove anything to anyone....

In some ways I had to be strong in order to not follow what everyone else was doing.

"Afraid to Learn" by Omar Morales is from *The Courage to Be Yourself: True Stories by Teens About Cliques, Conflicts, and Overcoming Peer Pressure*, used with permission from Free Spirit Publishing

Dealing with Rumors

CASEL SEL Competencies

SA Self-Awareness
SO Social Awareness

■ Agenda

Gathering: Telephone

Agenda Review

Activity 1: Small Group Work—Rumor Story

Activity 2: Go-Round—Sharing our Thoughts

Debriefing: How Is a Rumor Like a Tumor?

Closing: A Valuable Thing to Remember

■ Materials

Chart paper—one piece per group

Markers

Rumor Story handout—"Why Me?"

■ Prep

Put the Agenda on the board or on a chart

Make copies of the Rumor Story "Why Me?"—one per group

Write the discussion questions on the board, overhead, or on a chart

Gathering: Telephone

1. If possible, have students sit in a circle. Choose a student to begin the activity and whisper the statement, "If I had a penny for every rumor I heard, I'd be very, very wealthy." Students are to whisper the statement to the person sitting next to them as clearly as they can because students **cannot** ask for clarification or for the statement to be repeated if they did not hear it correctly. After the last person has heard the statement, ask him or her to repeat it to the class. Usually students are unsuccessful on the first try no matter how hard they attempt to listen correctly.

2. Try to track down when and how the statement mutated by asking several people from different places in the circle to share what they heard whispered to them.

3. Ask if they want to try again, and start with the statement, "Rumors hurt the target and create a hostile environment at school." This time, allow students to ask for clarification if they did not hear the statement clearly when it was whispered to them. Have the last person repeat the statement to the class. Again, share the original statement if it is different.

4. Ask the class:
    ⊙ What happened in this activity?
    ⊙ How were the two rounds different?
    ⊙ How is this activity like real life?

Agenda Review

Follow up on the previous questions by explaining that rumors are a kind of verbal bullying. It's categorized as "social bullying," which includes verbal threats and exclusion. Rumors and gossip are sometimes even more insidious than other types of bullying because the targets may not even hear the information being said about them, but can still suffer from the effects.

In the first Activity, we'll be reading "Why Me," a story about rumors, and, in small groups, begin to discuss the effects that rumors have for all of us. Then, we'll share those thoughts with the whole class, and focus especially on what we can do to prevent rumors and their sometimes devastating effects. The Debriefing will bring together all of our ideas, and the Closing will allow us to share what has affected us the most in this lesson.

Activity 1: Small Group Work—Rumor Story

1. Divide the class into several smaller groups (see the Teaching and Learning Strategies Appendix for suggestions on random grouping), and give each group copies of the rumor story, "Why Me?" and a piece of chart paper.

2. Ask that one person in the group read the story aloud. Then, the group should work together to answer the following questions, recording their answers on the chart paper.

    Questions:

    ⊙ How is the rumor spread in this story? What are other ways rumors are spread?

    ⊙ How do you think the rumor affected Tamara? Brainstorm a list of the effects of rumors on the target. How do rumors affect the school environment? Make a list.

    ⊙ Solve this math problem: Five students heard the rumor about Tamara before first period. During first period, each of these five students told five of their friends. How many people knew about the rumor by the end of first period? Each new person who heard the rumor told five friends in second period. How many students had heard the rumor by the end of second period? If this pattern continues (each person telling five friends in their next period class), how many students will know about the rumor by the end of fourth period?

      (Answer: $5 \times 5 = 25$ by the end of first period, $25 \times 5 = 125$ by the end of second period, $125 \times 5 = 625$ by the end of third, $625 \times 5 = 3125$ by the end of fourth period)

    ⊙ How can you personally stop rumors from spreading? What can schools do to stop rumors from spreading?

Activity 2: Go-Round—Sharing our Thoughts

1. In a go-round format, have each group answer question 1, "How is the rumor spread in this story? What are other ways rumors are spread?" In the next go-round, groups should answer question 2, "How do you think the rumor affected Tamara? How do rumors affect the school environment?" Next, have groups share their answers to the math problem.

2. In the last go-round, have groups share their answers to the fourth question, "How can you personally stop rumors from spreading? What can schools do to stop rumors from spreading?" As the groups share their answers, record them on a Top Ten Ways to Stop Rumors list on chart paper. Read the entire list back to the class after the groups have finished sharing.

Debriefing: How Is a Rumor Like a Tumor?

As a review, brainstorm the answers to two questions:

- How is a rumor like a tumor?
- How is stopping rumors like treating a tumor?

In her book *The Bully, the Bullied, and the Bystander,* Barbara Coloroso talks about the Sufis' "wisdom saying," which asks that our words pass through three gates: *Is it true?* If it isn't, don't say it. If it is true, it must pass through two more gates before you speak it: *Is it necessary to say?* and *Is it kind?* If it is not necessary to say it, don't say it. If it is necessary, say it in a kind way—one that allows the person to keep his/her self respect.

Closing: A Valuable Thing to Remember

Ask students to decide, in their groups, what they believe to be the most valuable thing to remember about the discussion today. Each group will share one thing.

> "*Rumors are like a snowball rolling down a mountain … as it rolls it picks up speed and more and more snow. Soon it creates an avalanche destroying people or places and then there is no going back.*"
>
> —FREDDY S. ZALTA

Rumor Story

"Why Me?"

Don't even get me started talking about rumors! They can ruin your life! Here's what happened to Tamara, one of my best friends, when some creeps started a rumor about her. We're both in 10th grade and in many of the same classes. I'm pretty outgoing and love talking to people (especially guys of course!), but Tamara is a bit shy around large groups of people. Neither of us have gone out on many dates. We mostly go to the movies or do other things with a large group of friends, both guys and girls. That's okay with both of us right now. Classes are tough this year, and I'm a cheerleader while Tamara's on the track team, so we don't actually have too much time for guys. I figure senior year there will be plenty of time for guys and prom and all that other fun stuff.

Anyway, there was this senior on the track team who kept asking Tamara to go out with him. He's pretty popular (and really good looking too!), and Tamara couldn't understand why he was asking her out. She thought maybe it was a joke or a dare from his friends. She just wasn't interested in him, so she said "no." Well, he wouldn't take "no" for an answer and kept asking. Finally, Tamara had enough and at practice one day, when he asked her out yet again, she said in a loud voice, "Look! Don't you get it? I'm not interested so back off!" Some of his buddies heard this and started to give the guy a hard time about it.

The next day after first period, we ran into one of our friends in the hallway. He looked at Tamara a little funny and asked if she had heard what was written about her in the guys' bathroom. It turns out that someone wrote all this sexual stuff about Tamara on the bathroom wall. It must have been that creep or one of his friends! By lunchtime it seemed like everyone in the school knew. Guys snickered and made rude gestures as Tamara walked by and some of the senior girls said, "Trying to get popular by sleeping with seniors?" Tamara burst into tears and ran out of math class when she saw a note being passed around asking who wanted to be next in line to sleep with Tamara.

The principal said he was sorry the incident had happened, but that the school couldn't very well repaint the bathrooms every time new graffiti appeared. So you can just imagine how the whole situation was out of control by the end of the week. Tamara started skipping track practice because she couldn't face the creep and skipped lunch too so she didn't have so many eyes staring at her. I wouldn't be surprised if she skips school next week. I'm really worried about her. She gets teary-eyed all the time and whispers, "Why me?" I'd like to hurt those guys like they hurt my friend!

Peer Pressure and Exclusion

CASEL SEL Competencies

SM Self-Management
SO Social Awareness
DM Responsible Decision-Making

■ Agenda

Gathering: Journal and Pair Share

Agenda Review

Activity 1: Mini Lecture—What Is Peer Pressure?

Activity 2: Opinion Poll—Types of Peer Pressure

Activity 3: Large Group Brainstorm—Statements to Say "No"

Activity 4: Concentric Circles—Practicing Resistance Statements

Debriefing

Closing: A Quote

■ Materials

Student journals or paper for journal writing

Chart paper with each peer pressure definition in Activity 1

Four signs labeled Positive Direct, Positive Indirect, Negative Indirect, and Negative Direct

Peer Pressure Cards

Handout—Peer Pressure Resistance Strategies: Ways to Say "No"

Gathering: Journal and Pair Share

1. Share this quote with students: "I, myself, started drinking because my friends drank and they started drinking because their friends drank also. I didn't even like beer when I first started drinking. But I had to fit in so I drank." Leslie Kaplan.

2. Ask students to write for 3 or 4 minutes about a time they chose to do something because of peer pressure.

3. Group students into pairs (see the Teaching and Learning Strategies Appendix for suggestions on random pairing). Give pairs 3 minutes to discuss their responses to the question, signaling when half of the time is up.

4. Bring the class back together and ask if any of their remembrances concerned positive behaviors. Perhaps they tried a new sport that they liked, because others were participating, or a new physical challenge, such as running a marathon. Very often, peer pressure is viewed as a negative, which is not necessarily true.

Agenda Review

Explain that this will be a time to explore peer pressure from a number of angles.

Peer pressure is something that everyone deals with. Most people like to be liked, and to fit in and be accepted. This need is one of the things that all teenagers struggle with and is a major part of growing up and becoming a young adult. Even older adults and students that we might consider popular struggle with peer pressure and the need to fit in. In the first Activity, we'll be identifying the types of peer pressure. Then, we'll be practicing identifying the four types that we define.

Explain that the next two activities will provide some opportunities to resist negative peer pressure, something that can seem hard to do sometimes.

In the Debriefing, we'll summarize our thoughts about resisting negative peer pressure, and then we'll close with our responses to a quotation.

Activity 1: Mini Lecture—What Is Peer Pressure?

1. Post the definition of peer pressure. *Peer pressure is when your friends or other people your age influence your behavior or actions.* Tell students that all people want to fit in and feel that they belong to a group. Because of that feeling, sometimes people do things they normally would not do in order to fit in. Explain that peer pressure can be positive or negative depending on what your friends are pressuring you to do.

2. Post the definition of direct peer pressure. *In direct peer pressure, you are specifically asked or pressured to do something that you may or may not want to do.* Direct peer pressure can be positive or negative. Ask students to give a few examples of direct peer pressure.

3. Post the definition of indirect peer pressure. In *indirect peer pressure, no one asks you directly to do something, but you still feel pressured to go along with the group.* Indirect peer pressure can be positive or negative. Positive indirect peer pressure can be an encouraging smile, gestures, or remarks; negative indirect peer pressure might take the form of dirty looks, rolling eyes, or derogatory remarks. Ask the group to give examples of both positive and negative indirect peer pressure.

4. Negative peer pressure might also take the form of excluding someone from the group if that person does not want to do what the group is doing. Ask students to give a few examples of times they have seen people excluded from a group as a result of peer pressure. Ask these two questions related to exclusion:

   ⊙ What does it feel like to be excluded from a group?

   ⊙ What might people do when they feel excluded? (Retaliate with violence, grades go down, etc.)

Activity 2: Opinion Poll—Types of Peer Pressure

1. Hang four signs in different parts of the room. The signs should be labeled Positive Direct, Positive Indirect, Negative Direct, and Negative Indirect.

2. Give each student a Peer Pressure Card. Students should read the card carefully and decide which type of peer pressure is described in the situation. Ask them to stand under the sign that illustrates the type of peer pressure described on the card. Ask for one or two volunteers under each sign to read their card and explain why they chose the sign they are standing under.

■ **Prep**

Place the Agenda on the board or on a chart

Write peer pressure definitions from Activity 1 on chart paper

Make the four signs labeled Positive Direct, Positive Indirect, Negative Indirect, and Negative Direct

Cut Peer Pressure Cards into strips

Make copies of the handout Resistance Strategies: Ways to Say "No"—one per student

Write the list of resistance strategies (from handout) on chart paper

Activity 3: Large Group Brainstorm—Statements to Say "No"

1. Distribute the handout Ways to Say "No." Invite students to take turns reading each out loud. The ways to say "no" are:
   - With a buddy
   - Change the subject
   - Remove yourself from the situation
   - Shift responsibility (i.e., "My coach says I can't")
   - Be direct and firm
   - With humor or a joke
   - Make an excuse
   - Give a reason
   - Invite the person to do something else
   - With creativity and imagination

2. After all of the ways have been read, go through the list again. For each way to say "no," ask students to give a specific statement they could use which reflects that strategy. For example:
   - Change the subject—"Hey, what did you think of that biology test?"
   - Shift responsibility—"No. My coach will kick me off the team if he finds out."
   - Give a reason—"No. I don't want to give my mom another reason to ground me."
   - Suggest an alternate activity—"Want to go to the mall?"

   Record all statements on chart paper for use in the next activity. Encourage students to write the statements on their handouts as people make suggestions.

3. Questions
   - Is it easy or difficult to stand up to peer pressure? Why?
   - Discuss what makes it easier to stand up to peer pressure (having a friend there, knowing how you will respond, etc.).
   - How can you let the people pressuring you know that you really mean "no"? What nonverbal messages need to go with your words?

4. Brainstorm a list of body language that's helpful in resisting negative peer pressure. The list could include such things as direct eye contact, standing up straight, crossing your arms, talking in a strong voice, etc. Record the list on chart paper for use in the next activity.

"I'm not in this world to live up to your expectations and you're not in this world to live up to mine."

—Bruce Lee

Activity 4: Concentric Circles—Practicing Resistance Statements

1. Have students stand in a large circle. Count off by two's. Two should step inside the circle and turn to face a 1 to form a pair. This sets up two circles, one inside of the other. If there is not a large open space in the room for a circle, modify the activity using rows of students instead of a circle. (For a more detailed description, see the Teaching and Learning Strategies Appendix.)

2. In the first round, the inside circle will try to pressure their partner in the outside circle to do something negative (smoke a cigarette, take a drink, spread rumors, steal, etc.). The outside circle will respond with a resistance statement reflecting the strategy for that rotation. Outside circle should use the following strategies:
   - Rotation 1: Change the subject
   - Rotation 2: Shift responsibility
   - Rotation 3: Give a reason or excuse
   - Rotation 4: Invite the person to do something else

3. Remind the outside circle to use body language that says "no." Announce the strategy for the rotation and give the pairs 30 seconds to complete the exchange.

4. Direct the outside circle to move two places to their right. Announce the next strategy and give the pairs 30 seconds to complete the exchange. Repeat this process two more times with the outside circle moving two places to the right each time.

5. Now the outside circle will try to pressure the inside circle. The inside circle will practice resistance statements using the same rotation pattern and process. Announce the rotation strategy (see above), give pairs 30 seconds, then instruct the inside circle to move two places to their right. Repeat this process with different strategies three more times.

Debriefing

Ask students to resume their seats and compliment them if they have done well.

Questions:
   - Was it easy or difficult to say "no"? Why?
   - What did you notice your partners doing well?
   - What do you think people should try to improve when they say "no"?

Closing: A Quote

Read the statement, "It's not my fault. My friends made me do it." Ask the group to share their thoughts and feelings about this quote. Ask what might be a better quote based on the information from this lesson.

Peer Pressure Cards

You and your friend are shopping in the mall. Your friend didn't bring much money, and she wants a new CD. She says to you, "Come on, just stick it in your jacket for me. If you were my friend you would do it."

— *What type of peer pressure is this?*

A good friend has decided to participate in a half marathon and is going to start training next week. She asks if you'd like to train with her.

— *What type of peer pressure is this?*

You notice two classmates talking in the hall between classes. You see them passing something that looks like cigarettes, and one winks at you and appears to beckon you over.

— *What type of peer pressure is this?*

Your class is working on group projects. Your group will be meeting after school to plan their presentation. You would prefer to go home and watch television, but you know the group is counting on you to attend.

— *What type of peer pressure is this?*

You've just started at a new school and have joined the soccer team. One day you see some of your teammates teasing a student in the hallway. You're kind of uncomfortable with the whole thing but think it must be a joke. Your teammates "accidentally" trip the girl and kick her books when she drops them. One of your teammates shouts to you, "Come on. Kick the books in the goal!"

— *What type of peer pressure is this?*

HANDOUT

You find a pack of cigarettes in your older brother's jacket. When you ask him about the cigarettes, he says he just smokes one or two to relax when he's hanging out with friends. He hands you a few cigarettes and the lighter.

— *What kind of peer pressure is this?*

You'd really like to get into better shape, but it seems as if all you do is talk about starting a fitness regimen. A friend has a set of free passes to the gym by your house and asks if you'd like to go twice a week.

— *What kind of peer pressure is this?*

A group from your school is going to work at the homeless shelter this weekend. This is something you've thought about doing, but just haven't gotten around to it. A notice is posted in your homeroom asking for volunteers.

— *What kind of peer pressure is this?*

Your best friend since 5th grade has really changed since you both started attending high school. Last week he invited you to a party with some of his new friends that starts at midnight. You ask him how he is going, since you know that he has the same curfew you do. He says he will wait until his parents are asleep and then sneak out. He does it all the time. You think, "Maybe I should go?"

— *What type of peer pressure is this?*

Peer Pressure Resistance Strategies: Ways to Say "No"

- ◉ Have a friend with you

- ◉ Change the subject

- ◉ Leave the situation—walk away

- ◉ Shift responsibility ("My coach says I can't")

- ◉ Be direct and firm

- ◉ Use humor or make a joke

- ◉ Make an excuse

- ◉ Give a reason

- ◉ Invite the person to do something else

- ◉ Use creativity and imagination ("I think I'm going to be sick. I gotta go!")

HANDOUT

Roles and Responses in Bullying and Harassment

CASEL SEL Competencies

SA Self-Awareness
RS Relationship Skills

■ Agenda

Gathering: Pairs

Agenda Review

Activity 1: Roles in Bullying and Harassment

Activity 2: Microlab—Dealing with Situations

Debriefing

Closing: New Learning

■ Materials

Handout—Dealing with Bullying and Harassment

■ Prep

Place the Agenda on the board or on a chart

If desired, chart the Roles in Bullying and Harassment in Activity 1. These may be used again in another lesson.

Make copies of the handout Dealing with Bullying and Harassment—one per student

Gathering: Pairs

1. Group students into pairs (see the Teaching and Learning Strategies Appendix for suggestions on random pairing). Give pairs 3 minutes to discuss these questions:
   - Have you ever been harassed or bullied? What happened?
   - How did you feel about it and how did it affect your life?
   - Did anyone come to your aid or support you?

2. Bring students back together and ask if any students would like to share their experiences with the class.

Agenda Review

Bullying and harassment are not new. However, views are changing about how serious this issue is, and now schools are responding to these issues as never before. Explain, "This lesson will be examining the roles people play in harassment and bullying, and begin to explore possible ways to deal with these issues. There is no one, perfect way to respond to any harassment or bullying; everyone needs to have a number of choices at their disposal.

"The Debriefing will provide a time for reflection about which responses you might be willing to try when involved in a situation, and the Closing will be a time to share a new thought or idea that you've had as a result of our work together."

Activity 1: Roles in Bullying and Harassment

1. Ask the class to brainstorm the different roles that people take in a bullying or harassment situation. List their responses on the board or on chart paper, and then compare them to the ones below:
   - **Target:** A person or group being harassed or bullied.
   - **Aggressor:** A person who taunts, threatens, humiliates, victimizes, or physically harms the target. Also known as a bully.
   - **Instigator:** A person who spreads rumors or gossip, or makes up things to encourage others to harass the target. Instigating can be done verbally, on the Internet, through instant messages, or through graffiti in public places. Not all bullying and harassment have an instigator. Sometimes the aggressor is responsible for these actions.

- **Bystander:** A person who either witnesses or knows the target is being harassed or bullied and does or says nothing. Bystanders may be adults or even a friend of the target.
- **Ally:** A person who stands up for the target by befriending her or him nonviolently and by challenging the aggressor's attacks.

2. Discuss what it means to be an ally. Emphasize that an ally is peaceful and nonviolent. Point out examples of peaceful and nonviolent struggles, such as the Civil Rights Movement of the 1950s – 1960s, when white, Latino, Native American, and other individuals allied with the African American community as they sought civil rights. What were some of the methods these allies used to help correct a social injustice or wrongdoing? (Mention some examples such as nonviolent marches, boycotts, standing up for victims, and speaking out against Jim Crow laws.)

3. Ask: How do these examples apply to harassment and bullying in schools?

4. Distribute the handout Dealing with Bullying and Harassment. Review with the class, perhaps asking students to read aloud. Ask the class to discuss the difficulty of intervening in situations like these. Explain that it takes practice to be assertive when targeted and when choosing to be an ally. There is no "right way" to respond; everyone needs to have many options at their disposal.

5. Students also need to understand that there are legal ramifications to harassment. Should harassment be proved, there are often harsh consequences for the aggressors. The federal government has outlined the legal obligations each school has to protect students from student-on-student racial and national-origin harassment, sexual and gender-based harassment, and disability harassment. Many states have also established additional laws to protect students.

Many times allies have a different relationship with the aggressor and can intervene successfully.

Activity 2: Microlab—Dealing with Situations

1. Divide the group into small groups of three (or four, if you'd like to combine the pairs used in the Gathering; the Teaching and Learning Strategies Appendix also provides a more detailed description of the microlab format).

2. Students will take turns responding to questions about harassment and bullying. Each person will have 60 seconds to respond to the question while the other two people listen carefully. Remind students that listening carefully means giving the speaker your full attention with no interrupting and no asking questions. Confidentiality is very important. Whatever is discussed in the microlab is to stay in the room. Students can decide how much information they want to share in the microlab. They do not need to disclose any information that would make them uncomfortable.

3. Groups should decide who will respond first. Read the first question, "Think about your first experience with bullying or harassment. What happened? Did you see someone being bullied? Were you bullied yourself? How old were you?" and allow 60 seconds for the first person to answer. Call time when 60 seconds is up and read the question again for the second person to answer, giving them 60 seconds. Do the same for the third person. Repeat this pattern for each of the four questions.

    Other questions for the microlab:

    ⊚ Why do you think people bully or harass others?

    ⊚ Have you ever been involved with "cyber-bullying" either with you as a target or as a witness to someone else being targeted? What happened? What was the outcome?

    ⊚ Was there anything in the handout we discussed that you found helpful? Which points?

4. After the final round, ask the following questions to the entire class:

    ⊚ What was this experience like for you? Was it easy or difficult? Why?

    ⊚ Why do you think people bully or harass others?

    ⊚ Have you ever been involved with "cyber-bullying" either with you as a target or as a witness to someone else being targeted? What happened? What was the outcome?

    ⊚ Was there anything in the handout we discussed that you found helpful? Which points?

Debriefing

Explain that the purpose of categorizing what happens in a bullying or harassment situation helps to be able to understand the dynamics involved in people's relationships with each other. Discussing how to respond gives us more choices when next we're confronted with bullying or harassment. Ask:

⊚ Are any of the strategies listed in the handout ones you use already?

⊚ Any that you feel you might like to try?

⊚ Which ones would take more practice to be comfortable with?

Closing: New Learning

Ask students to respond to these questions, popcorn-style (see the Teaching and Learning Strategies Appendix):

⊚ Did anything surprise you in the discussions we had today?

⊚ Is there any new learning you'll be taking away?

HANDOUT

Dealing with Bullying and Harassment

Here are a few things to consider when you confront or witness teasing, harassment, and bullying:

Ignoring isolated incidents may work, but a consistent problem of harassment will probably continue unless you act to stop it.

Many targets of harassment laugh at the beginning because they are nervous or embarrassed. They may believe or hope that they can just "laugh it off." Often aggressors and bystanders misinterpret the laughter, thinking it means the target doesn't mind.

When someone is harassing you, you can...

1. Stop what you're doing or saying and pause for a few seconds.

2. Think—What can I do or say that will help me take care of myself, send a strong message, and de-escalate the situation?

3. Say your message—
   - Say the person's name and show respect.
   - Say, "I don't like it when you_____. I want you to stop."

4. Exit—Don't wait for an apology or change of attitude. You said what you needed to say, and now you need to leave the scene, walk the other way, or focus your attention elsewhere.

5. If you choose to confront someone who is bullying or harassing you, find allies who will speak up, without using threats, to support you. This does not mean finding someone bigger to intimidate the aggressor, because this has the potential to escalate the problem. Many times allies have a different relationship with the aggressor and can intervene successfully.

Without allies, the cycle of harassment and bullying continues unchecked.

When someone is being harassed, you can be an ally when you...

1. Say the aggressor's name and show respect.

2. Name what you see, say why you don't like it, and tell the aggressor to STOP.

3. Take action...
   - Help the targeted person to leave the scene.
   - Go with the targeted person to report the incident.
   - Report the incident yourself.

It is especially effective if two or more allies speak up, because it helps to prevent the aggressor from turning on a single ally. If you see an ally who is getting picked on, act as an ally for that person and the target by saying something like, "This is getting really old. Can you just drop it already?"

From Bystander to Ally

CASE SEL Competencies

SM Self-Management
DM Responsible Decision-Making

■ Agenda

Gathering: Journal and Concentric Circles

Agenda Review

Activity 1: Role-Play Preparation

Activity 2: Role-Play Presentation

Debriefing

Closing: Pledge

■ Materials

Student journals or materials for student writing

Handout—Interrupting Harassment and Bullying: Guidelines for Allies

Handout—Role Play Scenarios

■ Prep

Place the agenda on the board or on a chart

Make copies of the handout Interrupting Harassment or Bullying: Guidelines for Allies—one for each student

Cut the Role-Play Scenarios handout into strips, one per group

If desired, chart the role-play guidelines and/or the goals of the role-plays outlined in Activity 1, #3

GATHERING: Journal and Concentric Circles

1. Write the quote by Edmund Burke on the board, or on chart paper, "All that is necessary for the triumph of evil is that good men do nothing." Ask students to write for three or four minutes about what they think the quote means.

2. Divide the class into two equal groups (if you don't have an equal number, you may join one). One group forms a circle, and then faces outward. The second group forms a second circle around the first one, facing in. Each person in the inner circle faces a partner in the outer circle. (If you don't have enough room to make circles, parallel rows will work. See Teaching and Learning for more explicit directions for Concentric Circles.) Explain that you will be posing a question and then each person will have about 45 seconds to share with their partner; all pairs will speak simultaneously. Identify whether the inside or outside person will speak first. After 45 seconds, you will signal that the other partner needs to begin to speak. When both partners have answered the first question, ask one of the circles to move two or three spaces to their right. Then pose the second question, and repeat the process. After that question, have the other circle move two places to their right.

    Questions:
    ⊙ What do you think the Edmund Burke quote means?
    ⊙ Listen to a second quote: "Strong people stand up for themselves. Stronger people stand up for others." Tell your partner what you think about this quote. Do you agree?
    ⊙ Tell your partner about a time when you stood up for someone else. Who was involved? What happened?

3. Bring the class back together and ask for any volunteers to comment on the three questions.

Agenda Review

We have talked a great deal about the issues of harassment and bullying, what we can do to deal with these issues, and how to stand up against unfair treatment of ourselves and others. Today we're going to prepare and present some role plays in which we put our skills to the test.

Explain that the class will be preparing role plays in Activity 1, using both a handout and their own creative ideas of how to be an effective ally. During the presentation of the role plays, the class will be identifying what strategies have been used, and exploring their effectiveness. The Debriefing is an opportunity to create an extensive list of strategies, so that they can become a part of a repertoire to use in our personal lives.

Explain that the Closing will provide a time for commitment to becoming an ally for others.

> *"All that is necessary for the triumph of evil is that good men do nothing."*
>
> EDMUND BURKE

Activity 1: Role Play Preparation

1. Distribute copies of the handout Interrupting Harassment or Bullying: Guidelines for Allies. Review the handout, and invite students to use the ideas in their role plays, and to add any they think would be effective. Remind students that allies confront the situation nonviolently.

2. Divide the class into six groups (see the Teaching and Learning Strategies Appendix for suggestions on random grouping) and give each small group one of the role play scenarios. In each scenario, the incident is reaching a crisis point where there will be a confrontation between the characters.

3. Each group should create a brief role play (3 minutes or less) that demonstrates what could happen in this confrontation if the ally helps the target and if the bystander has a change of heart and becomes an ally. The point of the role play is to show ways that allies and bystanders can stop harassment or bullying, or ways that targets can stand up for themselves. In their role plays, groups must:

   ◉ Briefly show what happens during the incident. This should be brief because the emphasis of the role play is on how to help the target, not on the harassment or bullying.

   ◉ Show the target trying to confront the aggressor or the instigator.

   ◉ Show the bystander watching the incident.

   ◉ Show the ally helping in some way.

   ◉ Show the bystander having a change of heart and starting to help.

Role Play Guidelines

   ◉ You can name the characters and add other details, as long as they do not detract from the main message of how to end the harassment or bullying. Names may not be people you know.

   ◉ Do not use bad language or any real physical violence.

   ◉ Emphasize how to be a good ally in the role play. Do not emphasize the harassment or bullying. It might be more fun to role play that part, but it is more important that you demonstrate how to be a good ally.

   ◉ The role play will be stopped if the guidelines are not followed.

[**Cautionary Note:** *Teachers or other adults should monitor the groups closely to make sure that students who are targets of harassment or bullying in real life are not forced to be targets in the role play. Teachers can assign the roles in each group if this is happening or is in danger of happening.*]

Activity 2: Role Play Presentation

1. Give each group 3 minutes to present their role-play to the large group. After each group's presentation, one of the group members should ask the large group these questions:
   - What type of harassment or bullying did you see in our role play?
   - What ally strategies did we demonstrate?

2. After all six groups have presented their role plays, briefly summarize the ally strategies demonstrated.

Debriefing

Ask:
- What did it feel like to act as an ally in the role plays?
- What did it feel like to be the target?
- How did it feel to have a change of heart as the bystander?

If groups have come up with additional effective comments, add them to the handout.

Closing: Pledge

Days after the shooting at Columbine High School in Littleton, Colorado, a group of Nashville, Tennessee, students created a pledge in order to take a stand against bullying and harassment.

They invited other students to sign the following pledge:

As part of my community and my school, I WILL:

- Pledge to be a part of the solution.
- Eliminate taunting from my own behavior.
- Encourage others to do the same.
- Do my part to make my community a safe place by being more sensitive to others.
- Set the example of a caring individual.
- Eliminate profanity toward others from my language.
- Not let my words or actions hurt others.
- And if others won't become a part of the solution, I WILL.

In a go-round, ask students to make one statement as a pledge.

> "Strong people stand up for themselves. Stronger people stand up for others."
>
> ANONYMOUS

Interrupting Harassment and Bullying: Guidelines for Allies

1. If you witness harassment, never enable the aggressor by laughing or stopping to just watch. Help the target by being a good ally. Speak up for him/her without putting anyone down. Try saying something like:
   - "Chill."
   - "Knock it off with the abusive language. No one deserves to hear that."
   - "I don't think that's funny."
   - "That's really cold—don't go there."
   - "Where did that come from? We don't say that kind of stuff here."
   - "That's just a rumor. Drop it."
   - "I saw that and it looked like harassment/bullying to me. Lay off."

   OTHER THINGS ALLIES COULD SAY …

   _____

   _____

   _____

   _____

2. When speaking to the person being harassed, say something like:
   - "I think they're being cruel."
   - "They're looking for trouble. This isn't worth it. Let's get out of here."
   - "You don't deserve this."

   OTHER THINGS ALLIES COULD SAY …

   _____

   _____

   _____

   _____

3. It is especially effective if two or more allies speak up, because it helps prevent the harasser or bully from turning on a single ally.

4. Take action. Help the target leave the scene. Go with the target to report the incident or report the incident yourself.

Role Play Scenarios

1. The teacher is handing out graded papers, and in the back of the room, the instigator is whispering to the aggressor about one of the students. They get louder, and finally the aggressor approaches the target and begins to make fun of his work and the grade he's received.

2. Two students are talking in the hallway when the target approaches. The instigator begins to question the target about something he/she has posted about the school, implying that the remarks are about the aggressor. Other students gather to listen, and the aggressor confronts the target with a threat.

3. A group of students are at a lunch table. The target approaches and the instigator begins to talk to the seated students about the target. When the target begins to sit down, the aggressor makes it clear that the student is not welcome.

4. As school is ending, students gather to talk, and the instigator shows a picture on his phone that he tells the aggressor has come from the target. The target has no idea what the picture is and begins to explain his innocence, when the aggressor begins to use threatening gestures and becomes angry.

5. During gym class, the target falls during an activity, and the class laughs. The instigator continues to point and make comments about the target, and finally the aggressor moves in and begins to mock the target.

6. A group of students are in the hallway, all talking about something they've read on Facebook the night before. The target approaches and everyone stops talking. The instigator begins to talk to the others about the postings that concern the target and something he/she is supposed to have done. The aggressor taunts the target about certain behaviors that are outlined in the posting.

GRADE 8
LESSONS ONE – SIX

Establishing a Safe, Respectful, and Supportive Environment

Setting the Stage for Learning about Bullying and Harassment

CASEL SEL Competencies

SA Self-Awareness
RS Relationship Skills

■ Agenda

Gathering: Concentric Circles

Agenda Review

Activity 1: Safe, Respectful, and Supportive Beings

Activity 2: Class Agreements

Debriefing

Closing: Easy and Hard

■ Materials

Chart paper—one sheet per group of four

Markers—a set per group

■ Prep

Place the Agenda on the board or on a chart

Gathering: Concentric Circles

1. This activity gives group members a chance to share with a variety of partners. Divide the class into two equal groups (if you don't have an equal number, you may join one). One group forms a circle, and then faces outward. The second group forms a second circle around the first one, facing in. Each person in the inner circle faces a partner in the outer circle. (If you don't have enough room to make circles, parallel rows will work. See the Teaching and Learning Strategies Appendix for more explicit directions for Concentric Circles.)

   Explain that you will be posing a question and then each person will have about 45 seconds to share with their partner; all pairs will speak simultaneously. Identify whether the inside or outside person will speak first. After 45 seconds, you will signal that the other partner needs to begin to speak. When both partners have answered the first question, ask one of the circles to move two or three spaces to their right. Then pose the second question, and repeat the process. After that question, have the other circle move two places to their right.

   Questions:
   ⊚ Ask students to think about a time when they were part of a group and felt respected, cared for, and safe being themselves. It may have been a particular class in school, or some other group with whom they worked. What was it about that experience that made them feel respected, cared for, and safe to be who they are?

   ⊚ Thinking again back to that positive group experience, try to be specific about how the members of the group treated each other. What were specific things people did or did not do?

   ⊚ Last question about that productive environment you've been describing: How did people in the group show that they respected each other? Were there certain actions or words that showed respect? How does one show respect for another person?

2. Thank the students for participating in the Gathering and ask them to take their seats. Ask if anyone would like to tell the group anything that came up during the Gathering that surprised them.

Agenda Review

Explain that, just as they began to explore in the Gathering, today's lesson will give them an opportunity to talk more about being respected, safe and supported. As the Agenda shows, we'll be doing an activity called Safe, Respectful, and Supportive Beings. This will help us create some Agreements about how we'd like to be treated in this classroom, particularly as we begin to talk about the sensitive issues of harassment and bullying.

The Debriefing will help us to look at our Agreements and think about how to keep them. We'll close with some thoughts about making the Agreements real.

Activity 1: Safe, Respectful, and Supportive Beings

1. Draw a gingerbread person shape on the board, or any shape that will provide a "Being." Perhaps your school has a mascot, or you may have a local sports team, etc.

2. Ask students to reflect back on the Gathering and ask what actions, ways of treating each other, and attitudes would make the classroom a place where everyone would feel included and respected.

3. Write the positive things they brainstorm *inside* the outline of the Being. Some possible things to include might be listening, disagreeing respectfully, etc.

4. If negative items begin to come up, begin to place these things *outside* the outline of the Being. This will reflect the actions, ways of interacting, and attitudes that they do *not* want as part of the classroom environment, such as name-calling, etc.

5. Feel comfortable in adding your own ideas within the Being, as you are a member of the group as well. Strive to avoid a lecturing tone, however.

Activity 2: Class Agreements

1. Explain: Now that we've had a chance to explore this topic, we'll use this information to create some Class Agreements to ensure that these actions and behaviors become a part of our classroom.

2. Label a piece of chart paper "Class Agreements."

3. Ask students to think about what was placed in the Being and brainstorm Agreements, such as "practice good listening." You might pause after suggestions that are broad in scope, and take a moment to be specific (for example, "What makes a good listener?" or "How does someone show 'respect'?" Many of these items are culturally linked, and are not universally practiced in the same way. These specifics can be noted on an additional paper, listed on the board as you go, or taught as separate lessons (see the Resources Appendix for additional curricula).

4. After everyone has contributed, ask if there are any Agreements that can be combined because they are similar. Make sure that students understand that you are grouping similar ideas, not changing their words.

5. Once each suggestion has been refined into an Agreement, ask students if they can agree to that guideline. Keep in mind that you are working to a consensus, so avoid a voting situation.

Debriefing

Read over the list of Agreements the class has created.

Ask:
- How do you think these Agreements will help our class be supportive and encouraging?
- Is there a way we can be gently reminded when we forget to adhere to the Agreements?

Students sometimes come up with harsh punishment because that is what they've heard elsewhere. Point out that it is helpful to practice kind ways to remind others about unfavorable behavior and to say things such as, "I don't like it when you say ___. We agreed that we would be respectful, and that doesn't feel respectful to me."

Closing: Easy and Hard

Ask students to respond to these questions, popcorn-style (see the Teaching and Learning Strategies Appendix).

- What is something that will be easy for you to adhere to in the Agreements we just created?
- What is something that might be harder?

It is helpful to practice kind ways to remind others about unfavorable behavior.

Identifying Harassment and Bullying

CASEL SEL Competencies

SA Self-Awareness
SO Social Awareness
RS Relationship Skills

■ Agenda

Gathering: Web
Agenda Review
Activity: Microlab on Bullying and Harassment
Debriefing
Closing: New Learning

■ Materials

Materials to get students into microlab groups (see the Teaching and Learning Strategies Appendix)

■ Prep

Place the Agenda on the board or on a chart

Gathering: Web

Write the words "harassment" and "bullying" in the center of the board or on a piece of chart paper. Ask students what words or phrases come to mind when they see these two words. Add their contributed words to the board or chart paper with lines stemming out from the word in the center. You may choose to cluster like responses together. (See the Teaching and Learning Strategies Appendix for further information on webbing.)

Agenda Review

Explain that, as can be seen from the Gathering Web, these two words—harassment and bullying—can have different meanings for people. In today's Activity, students will have the opportunity to talk about these issues and their experiences and opinions. The Debriefing will allow the whole group to reflect on these experiences, and the Closing will invite students to share their thoughts on how the Activity might have opened them up to some new thoughts.

Activity: Microlab on Bullying and Harassment

1. Divide the group into small groups of three. (See the Teaching and Learning Strategies Appendix for suggestions on random grouping. This is particularly important to do in beginning lessons, as it sets the stage for random grouping each time students participate in a lesson. Once they get used to this method, it becomes easier to get students to speak with others whom they may not know well. The Teaching and Learning Strategies Appendix also provides a more extensive description of the microlab format.)

2. Students will take turns responding to questions about harassment and bullying. Each person will have 60 seconds to respond to the question while the other two people listen carefully. Remind students that listening carefully means giving the speaker your full attention with no interrupting and no asking questions. Confidentiality is very important. Whatever is discussed in the microlab is to stay in the room. Students can decide how much information they want to share in the microlab. They do not need to disclose any information that would make them uncomfortable.

3. Groups should decide who will respond first. Read the first question, "Think about your first experience with bullying or harassment. What happened? Did you see someone being bullied? Were you bullied yourself? How old were you?" and allow 60 seconds for the first person to answer. Call time when 60 seconds is up and read the question again for the second person to answer, giving them 60 seconds. Do the same for the third person. Repeat this pattern for each of the four remaining questions.

Additional questions for the microlab:
- Why do people bully or harass others?
- What does your family say about bullying and harassment?
- What do the media (television, movies, video games, magazines, the Internet) say about bullying and harassment? Is this the same or different than what your family says?
- Do you think harassment in schools is getting worse or better? Why?

Debriefing

1. After the final round, debrief the experience in a large group discussion using the following questions:
   - What was this experience like for you? Was it easy or difficult? Why?
   - Why do people bully or harass others?
   - What do your families say about bullying and harassment?
   - What do the media say about bullying and harassment?
   - Do you think harassment in schools is getting worse or better? Why?

2. You might also explain that bullying can be differentiated from harassment. Harassment is linked to aspects of one's identity, e.g. gender, race, sexual orientation, etc.

3. If the topic does not arise from the discussion, explain to students that "cyber-bullying" is a term for acts such as these that occur using the Internet or other digital technologies. In the last few years, it has become as great a concern as traditional bullying, and perhaps greater according to some statistical data. According to the Fall 2010 issue of *Teaching Tolerance*, anywhere from one-third to one-half of youths have been targeted by cyber-bullies. Incidents of online bullying have led to documented incidents of "bullycide," students who take their own lives as a result of the torment from others.

4. Explain that students will have the opportunity to talk more about appropriate responses to bullying and harassment in later lessons.

Closing: New Learning

Ask students to respond to these questions, popcorn-style (see the Teaching and Learning Strategies Appendix):

- Did anything surprise you in the discussions we had today?
- Is there any new learning you'll be taking away?

"Never bend your head. Always hold it high. Look the world right in the eye."

—Helen Keller

The Power of Cliques

CASEL SEL Competencies

SO Social Awareness
RS Relationship Skills

■ Agenda

Gathering: Go-Round

Agenda Review

Activity 1: "Which Crowd Did You Pick?" by Satra Wasserman

Activity 2: Mapping the Groups in School

Debriefing

Closing: Now I Know

■ Materials

Handout — "Which Crowd Did You Pick?"

Chart paper—one piece for each group of four or five students

Markers—one set per group

■ Prep

Place the Agenda on the board or on a chart

Gathering: Go-Round

In a go-round, ask students to complete this sentence, "One of my favorite things to do in the world is to ___." Contribute your own answer as well.

Agenda Review

Point out to students that there were both similarities and differences in the things we love to do. It is because of this diversity that life is so interesting. If we were all the same, how boring it would be! People generally like to spend time with others who share things in common with them. Young people very often hang out in groups at school with others who are like them, or like to do the things they do.

The topic today is cliques—defined by one dictionary as "a narrow exclusive circle or group of persons; one held together by common interests, views, or purposes."

Explain that this lesson will explore the issue of how and why young people belong to groups, and what impact group membership has on them.

Say, "We'll be reading "Which Crowd Did You Pick?" and discussing its implications. Then, we'll be mapping the groups we see in our school in our second Activity. The Debriefing will be concerned with the impact of the groups, and the Closing with a sharing of new awareness this discussion has provided for us."

Activity 1: "Which Crowd Did You Pick?"

1. Read aloud, "Which Crowd Did You Pick?" by Satra Wasserman from *The Courage to Be Yourself: True Stories by Teens About Cliques, Conflicts, and Overcoming Peer Pressure*, or ask for volunteers to read several paragraphs, which is short enough that this should take only a few minutes. Ask for volunteers to summarize the story in two or three sentences.

2. Divide the class into groups of four or five (see the Teaching and Learning Strategies Appendix for ideas for random pairing). Put the first of the following questions on the board or chart paper and give the groups 2–3 minutes to discuss it. Then put the next question up, again allowing 2–3 minutes for small group discussion. Finally put the third question up for discussion.

   ⊙ Why did Satra's basketball friends exile him?

   ⊙ Have you ever been in a similar situation? If so, describe it.

   ⊙ What are the cliques in our school? Can you describe what they wear, the music they listen to, or other things about them?

Activity 2: Mapping the Groups in School

1. Hand out chart paper and markers to each group. Ask the groups to draw a map of the school that indicates where various cliques hang out in or around the school. The maps can show the interior of the school, such as the lunchroom, in addition to the areas outside the school where kids congregate by groups. On the map, group members should describe the cliques, including their dress, behavior, or other distinguishing features.

2. Allow 10-12 minutes for the mapping activity. When time is up, post the maps on the board or around the room, or allow students to circulate in the room to compare all the different versions of the maps.

Debriefing

Conduct a large group discussion around the following questions:

- In what ways are the maps and descriptions of groups similar to and different from each other?
- Can a person belong to more than one group? Do you?
- How do other groups stereotype your group?
- Do people in different groups mingle? If not, why not?
- In what ways do labels and cliques limit or harm people? Can or should anything be done to prevent people from breaking apart into cliques, or isolating those who are different?

Closing: Now I Know

Ask: How did these activities change your view of groups, either one you belong to or groups in general? Place the following sentences on the board and ask for volunteers to complete them: Before this discussion, I didn't know ___. After this discussion, I know ___.

"Remember the first day of school, looking at all the kids, saying to yourself, who am I going to hang with?"

—Satra Wasserman

"Which Crowd Did You Pick?"
by Satra Wasserman

Remember the first day of school, looking at all the kids, saying to yourself, "Who am I going to hang with?" Which crowd did you pick?

If your school is like the one I used to go to, you can probably draw a map of the lunchroom or of the sidewalk out front, with different colored areas to indicate all the different cliques and where they hang out.

On one corner are the jocks. Over yonder is the hip-hop crowd. Across the street are the nerds.

Then you have the rich kids with their latest fashions, the not-so-rich kids on their skateboards. And the list goes on and on.

I realize that at many schools the list wouldn't be this long, but at my high school it was.

In the first few months of my freshman year, I was down with the basketball team. I knew the whole squad. We would play basketball in gym class, we'd all sweat the same girls, and we'd talk about how funny looking our classmates were.

From September until springtime it was all good. Then JV basketball tryouts came around and I didn't show up. These guys couldn't believe it. "Yo Sat, where were you?" they asked.

I told them basketball was cool, but that handball was my new game. It only took about one day for the reality of this to sink in with my new friends. "Satra, you're playing handball with those weird kids?" they asked in disbelief. Then I was exiled.

Before, we would chill with each other all the time. Then, almost overnight, if I saw the guys from the basketball team in the hallways, they would act like we didn't know each other. Two years went by before I talked with any of them again. This is just one example of what happens with cliques.

"Which Crowd Did You Pick?" by Satra Wasserman is from *The Courage to Be Yourself: True Stories by Teens About Cliques, Conflicts, and Overcoming Peer Pressure*, used with permission from Free Spirit Publishing

Understanding Peer Pressure

CASEL SEL Competencies

SO Social Awareness
RS Relationship Skills

■ Agenda

Gathering: Pair Share—A Time You Experienced Peer Pressure

Agenda Review

Activity 1: Mini Lecture—What is Peer Pressure?

Activity 2: Role Play Preparation

Activity 3: Role Play Presentations

Debriefing

Closing: What Works Best?

■ Materials

Chart paper with each peer pressure definition from Activity 1

Handout—Peer Pressure Resistance Strategies: Ways to Say "No"

Handout—Peer Pressure Scenarios

■ Prep

Place the Agenda on the board or on a chart

Write peer pressure definitions from Activity 1 on chart paper

Make copies of the handout Peer Pressure Resistance Strategies: Ways to Say "No"—one per student

Write the list of resistance strategies (from handout) on chart paper

Make one copy of Peer Pressure Scenarios and cut into strips

Gathering: Pair Share—A Time You Experienced Peer Pressure

1. Group students into pairs (see the Teaching and Learning Strategies Appendix for suggestions on random pairing).

2. Explain that everyone has had the experience of being influenced by others in their group. These pressures can have good outcomes and bad outcomes. Invite students to think about a time a friend pressured them to do something positive (i.e., study for an exam, help a teacher, etc.) and what he/she did in the situation. The second part of the instruction is to think about a time a friend pressured them to do something negative (i.e. smoking, cheating, etc.) and what they decided to do in that situation.

3. The first person will address these questions for 2 minutes. You will signal when 2 minutes are up, and it will be time for the second person to talk.

4. Debrief the activity with these questions:
   ⊙ What did it feel like when your friend pressured you to do something positive?
   ⊙ Negative?
   ⊙ What did you decide to do in each situation?
   ⊙ How did you decide what to do (think of your values, consider the consequences, etc.)?

Agenda Review

The lesson today concerns this complicated issue of peer pressure. Explain that in the first Activity, some time will be devoted to creating some definitions for kinds of peer pressure. The second Activity will introduce some ways to say "no" to negative peer pressure and some practice in groups.

The Debriefing will be a time to synthesize what we've explored, and during the Closing we'll share what might work best for us personally.

Activity 1: Mini Lecture—What Is Peer Pressure?

1. Post the definition of peer pressure. *Peer pressure is when your friends or other people your age influence your behavior or actions.* Tell students that all people want to fit in and feel that they belong to a group. Because of that feeling, sometimes people do things they normally would not do in order to fit in. Explain that peer pressure can be positive or negative depending on what your friends are pressuring you to do.

2. Post the definition of direct peer pressure. In *direct peer pressure, you are specifically asked or pressured to do something that you may or may not want to do.* Direct peer pressure can be *positive* or *negative*. Ask students to give a few examples of direct peer pressure.

3. Post the definition of indirect peer pressure. In *indirect peer pressure, no one asks you directly to do something but you still feel pressured to go along with the group.* Indirect peer pressure can be positive or negative. Positive indirect peer pressure can be an encouraging smile, gestures, or remarks; negative indirect peer pressure might take the form of dirty looks, rolling eyes, or derogatory remarks. Ask the group to give examples of both positive and negative indirect peer pressure.

4. Negative peer pressure might also take the form of excluding someone from the group if that person does not want to do what the group is doing. Ask students to give a few examples of times they have seen people excluded from a group as a result of peer pressure.

5. Ask these two questions related to exclusion:
    *   What does it feel like to be excluded from a group?
    *   What might people do when they feel excluded? (retaliate with violence, grades go down, etc.)

Activity 2: Role Play Preparation

1. Explain that although it can be easy to identify examples of peer pressure, it is often difficult to deal with peer pressure in real-life situations. The next activity will provide practice dealing with peer pressure situations.

2. Divide the class into five to eight groups (suggestions for random grouping can be found in the Teaching and Learning Strategies Appendix. If you randomly grouped for the Gathering, you might join pairs to make groups of four).

3. Distribute the handout—Peer Pressure Resistance Strategies: Ways to Say "No." Explain that these ideas will be useful as they create role plays with their groups.

4. Distribute a peer pressure scenario to each group. Explain that their challenge is to design and demonstrate a role play for the larger group that illustrates at least two ways to say "no" in that particular peer pressure situation. Groups should remember to demonstrate body language that says "no" in addition to the resistance strategies.

Activity 3: Role Play Presentations

Give groups 3 minutes to present their role play. Someone in the small group should ask the audience the following questions after their role play:

- ◎ What type of peer pressure did you see?
- ◎ Which refusal skills did we use?
- ◎ What did you like about how we handled the situation? What did we do well?

Debriefing

1. With the class reassembled, ask how the experience felt to practice these refusal skills. Did you feel that the role plays were realistic? Why or why not?

2. Read the statement, "It's not my fault. My friends made me do it." Ask the group the following questions:
   - ◎ How did the role plays prove that this statement is not true?
   - ◎ Why do people say, "It's not my fault. My friends made me do it."?

3. Explain that a role play can feel uncomfortable because the situation isn't actually real. However, practice allows us to get better, just as it does with any new skill. Also, there is no "one right way" to communicate with others; we all need to find out what works for us.

Closing: What Works Best?

Ask students to share, popcorn-style (see the Teaching and Learning Strategies Appendix), which of the refusal skills seem to work best for them.

"Rarely do schools acknowledge the power of peer culture in defining standards, and rarely do they take advantage of this power as an engine for quality."

—Ron Berger

Peer Pressure Resistance Strategies:
Ways to Say "No"

- Have a friend with you

- Change the subject

- Leave the situation—walk away

- Shift responsibility ("My coach says I can't")

- Be direct and firm

- Use humor or make a joke

- Make an excuse

- Give a reason

- Invite the person to do something else

- Use creativity and imagination ("I think I'm going to be sick. I gotta go!")

HANDOUT

Peer Pressure Scenarios

Scenario 1

You and your friend are shopping in the mall. You know your friend occasionally "lifts" things from stores, but she has never done so when you have been together. While in a music store, she sees a CD of a hot new group that she would like to buy. After checking her wallet, she realizes that she does not have enough money for the CD. She says to you, "Come on, just stick it in your jacket for me. If you were my friend you would do it."

What type of peer pressure is this? What do you do? What are two ways to say "no" in this situation?

Scenario 2

You are attending a party given by some college kids. Your best friend has been invited because one of the guys giving the party is dating his sister. You and he feel pretty lucky to attend. It is supposed to be a "dry" party (no alcohol), but later you and your friend notice that some of the older guys and girls are definitely drinking and are smoking pot. Your friend says, "Let's just have one drink to loosen up a bit."

What type of peer pressure is this? What do you do? What are two ways to say "no" in this situation?

Scenario 3

Things have been pretty tense at school lately. Some of the different groups have been bickering more than usual in the cafeteria—throwing food across tables and yelling insults at each other. You heard a few guys in your gym class saying that thcy arc going to "get them back." As you are putting on your gym shoes you see a group of them huddled talking and laughing and then you hear a click. They look up and see you watching so they gesture you to come over and join them.

What type of peer pressure is this? What do you do? What are two ways to say "no" in this situation?

Scenario 4

You are attending a party with a group of three friends. You are driving your mom's car and have chosen not to drink. On the way home, your best friend, who has been drinking, keeps telling you to drive faster, faster, saying, "You drive like an old woman!"

What type of peer pressure is this? What do you do? What are two ways to say "no" in this situation?

Scenario 5

You've just started at a new school and have joined the soccer team. One day you see some of your teammates teasing a student in the hallway. You're kind of uncomfortable with the whole thing but think it must be a joke. Your teammates "accidentally" trip the girl and kick her books when she drops them. One of your teammates shouts to you, "Come on. Kick the books in the goal!

What type of peer pressure is this? What do you do? What are two ways to say "no" in this situation?

Scenario 6

You find a pack of cigarettes in your older brother's jacket. When you ask him about the cigarettes, he says he just smokes one or two to relax when he's hanging out with friends. He hands you a few cigarettes and the lighter.

What kind of peer pressure is this? What do you do? What are two ways to say "no" in this situation?

Scenario 7

You really want to be on the swim team, and the lifeguard at the YMCA says that she thinks you should give it a try. You try out and are one minute slower than the other people trying out. Disappointed, you start to compare their times, form, and body type to yours. One girl tells you that, "These pills helped me take off a few pounds. Maybe they could help you too." You think, "If she can do it, so can I. Maybe I can cut my time by taking pills to slim down."

What type of peer pressure is this? What do you do? What are two ways to say "no" in this situation?

Scenario 8

Your best friend since 5th grade has really changed since you both started attending high school. Last week he invited you to a party with some of his new friends that starts at midnight. You ask him how he is going, since you know that he has the same curfew you do. He says he will wait until his parents are asleep and then sneak out. He does it all the time. You think, "Maybe I should go?"

What type of peer pressure is this? What do you do? What are two ways to say "no" in this situation?

Roles and Responses in Bullying and Harassment

CASEL SEL Competencies

RS Relationships Skills
DM Responsible Decision-Making

■ Agenda

Gathering: "The Bully" by Roger Dean Kiser

Agenda Review

Activity 1: Roles in Bullying and Harassment

Activity 2: Rotation Stations— Questioning Roles

Debriefing

Closing: Thinking About ____

■ Materials

Handout—"The Bully" by Roger Dean Kiser

Chart paper—one piece for each of five groups

One set of markers for each group

Handout—Responding to Bullying and Harassment: Guidelines for Targets

Handout—Responding to Bullying and Harassment: Guidelines for Allies

Gathering: "The Bully"

1. Read the story "The Bully" by Roger Dean Kiser

2. Group students into pairs (see the Teaching and Learning Strategies Appendix for suggestions on random pairing). Give pairs 3 minutes to discuss these questions:

    ◉ Have you ever been teased or harassed?

    ◉ What feelings did that trigger and how did it affect your life?

    ◉ Roger Kiser had no friends to support him. Did you? Did anyone intervene on your behalf?

Agenda Review

Bullying and harassment are not new. However, with the advent of technology it has been amplified, and now schools are responding to these issues as never before. Explain that this lesson will be examining the roles people play in harassment and bullying, and beginning to explore possible ways to deal with these issues. There is no one, perfect way to respond to any harassment or bullying; everyone needs to have a number of choices at their disposal.

The Debriefing will bring all of our brainstorming together, and the Closing will be a time to share a new thought or idea that you've had as a result of our work together.

Activity 1: Roles in Bullying and Harassment

1. Ask the class to brainstorm the different roles that people take in a bullying or harassment situation. List their responses on the board or on chart paper, and then compare them to the ones below:

    ◉ **Target:** A person or group being harassed or bullied.

    ◉ **Aggressor:** A person who taunts, threatens, humiliates, victimizes, or physically harms the target. Also known as a bully.

    ◉ **Instigator:** A person who spreads rumors, gossip, or makes up things to encourage others to harass the target. Instigating can be done verbally, on the Internet, through instant messages, or through graffiti in public places. Not all bullying and harassment have an instigator. Sometimes the aggressor is responsible for these actions.

- **Bystander:** A person who either witnesses or knows the target is being harassed or bullied and does or says nothing. Bystanders may be adults or even a friend of the target.
- **Ally:** A person who stands up for the target by befriending her or him nonviolently and by challenging the aggressor's attacks.

2. Discuss what it means to be an ally. Emphasize that an ally is peaceful and nonviolent. Point out examples of peaceful and nonviolent struggles, such as the Civil Rights Movement of the 1950s – 1960s, when white, Latino, Native American, and other individuals allied with the African American community as they sought civil rights. What were some of the methods these allies used to help correct a social injustice or wrongdoing? (Mention some examples such as nonviolent marches, boycotts, standing up for victims, and speaking out against Jim Crow laws.)

- How do these examples apply to harassment and bullying in schools?

Activity 2: Rotation Stations—Questioning Roles

1. Divide the class into five groups (see the Teaching and Learning Strategies Appendix for random grouping ideas, as well as a description of Rotation Stations) and direct each group to stand at one of the areas you have designated. Give each group a piece of chart paper that has one of the following questions written on it:

- What can targets do when they are being harassed or bullied? Where can they get help?
- What kinds of consequences should there be for aggressors at school?
- Why do people become instigators? What can you do to prevent people from instigating conflict and social drama?
- How can bystanders become allies?
- How can allies confront instigators and work to educate the school about bullying and harassment?

2. Allow 2 minutes or so for the group to brainstorm responses to their question and record them on the chart paper. At the end of the time, have all of the groups rotate to another station, leaving their chart paper behind. At their new stations, groups should take another 2 minutes or so to read the question and add their responses to the list started by the previous group. Continue until all of the groups have comments on all of the stations, and have returned to their original question(s).

3. Ask volunteers from each group to read the question(s) and responses out loud to the class. Discuss the fact that most people play more than one of these roles every day. For example, a person may act as an ally in one circumstance but as an instigator when in a different crowd. (Note: If some of the responses are not nonviolent, remind students of the definition of an ally.)

Prep

Place the Agenda on the board or on a chart

If desired, chart the Roles in Bullying and Harassment in Activity 1

Write one question from Activity 2 on each of the five pieces of chart paper

If desired, make copies of "The Bully" for students

Make copies of the handout Responding to Bullying and Harassment: Guidelines for Targets —one per student

Make copies of the handout Responding to Bullying and Harassment: Guidelines for Allies —one per student

Debriefing

1. Distribute the handouts—Responding to Bullying and Harassment: Guidelines for Targets and Responding to Bullying and Harassment: Guidelines for Allies.

2. Discuss after students have read silently, or ask for volunteers to read sections. Ask for any comments. (Note: If students comment that some of the suggestions wouldn't work for them, acknowledge that everyone needs to feel comfortable with the choices they make in dealing with this difficult issue. However, with practice, more choices can become easier to use. Certainly if the environment values dealing with bullying and harassment, and refuses to ignore them, more people will feel comfortable in speaking up.)

3. Students also need to understand that there are legal ramifications to harassment. Should harassment be proved, there are often harsh consequences for the aggressors. The federal government has outlined the legal obligations each school has to protect students from student-on-student racial and national-origin harassment, sexual and gender-based harassment, and disability harassment. Many states have also established additional laws to protect students.

Closing: Thinking About ___

In a go-round (see the Teaching and Learning Strategies Appendix), ask students to complete the following sentence. Begin by sharing your own answer. As we worked together, I kept thinking about ___

Bullying and harassment are not new. However, with the advent of technology it has been amplified.

"The Bully"
by Roger Dean Kiser

I walked into the Huddle House restaurant in Brunswick, Georgia and sat down at the counter as all of the booths were taken. I picked up a menu and began to look at the various items trying to decide if I wanted to order breakfast or just go ahead and eat lunch.

"Excuse me," said someone, as they touched me on the shoulder.

I looked up and turned to the side to see a rather nice looking woman standing before me.

"Is your name Roger by any chance?" she asked me.

"Yes." I responded, looking rather confused as I had never seen the woman before.

"My name is Barbara and my husband is Tony," she said, pointing to a distant table near the door leading into the bathrooms.

I looked in the direction that she was pointing but I did not recognize the man who was sitting, alone at the table.

"I'm sorry. I'm, ah. I'm ah, confused. I don't think that I know you guys. But my name is Roger. Roger Kiser," I told her.

"Tony Claxton. Tony from Landon High School in Jacksonville, Florida?" she asked me.

"I'm really sorry. The name doesn't ring a bell," I said.

She turned and walked back to her table and sat down. She and her husband immediately began talking and once in a while I would see her turn around in her seat and look directly at me.

I finally decided to order breakfast and a cup of decaffeinated coffee. I sat there continually racking my brain trying to remember who this Tony guy was.

"I must know him," I thought to myself. "He recognizes me for some reason." I picked up my coffee up and took a sip. All of a sudden it came to me like a flash of lighting.

"Tony. TONY THE BULL," I mumbled, as I swung myself around on my stool and faced in his direction.

"The bully of my seventh grade geography class," I thought.

How many times that sorry guy had made fun of my big ears in front of the girls in my class? How many times this sorry son-of-a-gun had laughed at me because I had no parents and had to live in an orphanage? How many times had this big bully slammed me up against the lockers in the hallway just to make himself look like a big man to all the other students?

He raised his hand and waved at me. I smiled, returned the wave, and turned back around and began to eat my breakfast.

"Jesus. He's so thin now. Not the big burly guy that I remember from back in 1957," I thought to myself.

All of a sudden I heard the sound of dishes breaking so I spun around to see what had happened. Tony had accidentally hit several plates, knocking them off the table as he was trying to get into his wheelchair which had been parked in the bathroom hallway while they were eating. The waitress ran over and started picking up the broken dishes and I listened as Tony and his wife tried to apologize.

HANDOUT

As Tony rolled by me, being pushed by his wife, I looked up and I smiled.

"Roger," he said, as he nodded his head forward.

"Tony," I responded, as I nodded my head, in return.

I watched as they went out of the door and slowly made their way to a large van which had a wheelchair loader located in the side door of the vehicle.

I sat and watched as his wife tried, over and over, to get the ramp to come down. But it just would not work. Finally I got up, paid for my meal, and I walked up to the van.

"What's the problem?" I asked.

"Darn thing sticks once in a while," said Tony. "Could you help me get him in the van?" asked his wife.

"I think I can do that," I said as I grabbed the wheelchair and rolled Tony over to the passenger door.

I opened the door and locked the brakes on the wheelchair.

"OK. Arms around the neck, Dude," I said as I reached down and grabbed him around the waist and carefully raised him up into the passenger seat of the van.

As Tony let go of my neck I reached over and swung his limp, lifeless legs, one at a time, into the van so that they would be stationed directly in front of him.

"You remember. Don't you?" he said, looking directly into my eyes.

"I remember, Tony," I said.

"I guess you're thinking 'What goes around comes around'," he said, softly.

"I would never think like that, Tony," I said, with a stern look on my face.

He reached over and grabbed both of my hands and squeezed them tightly.

"Is how I feel in this wheelchair how you felt way back then when you lived in the orphan home?" he asked me.

"Almost, Tony. You are very lucky. You have someone to push you around who loves you. I didn't have anyone," I responded.

I reached in my pocket and pulled out one of my cards that had my home telephone number written on it, and I handed it to him.

"Give me a call sometime. We'll do lunch," I told him. We both laughed.

I stood there watching as they drove toward the interstate and finally disappeared onto the southbound ramp. I hope he calls me sometime. He will be the only friend that I have from my high school days.

Responding to Bullying and Harassment: Guidelines for Targets

Ignoring isolated incidents may work, but a consistent problem of harassment will probably continue unless you act to stop it.

You might try to respond in the following ways:

1. Say the aggressor's name and show respect. Sometimes this means saying something like, "Steven, I don't mean any disrespect. I just want you to know…"

2. Tell the aggressor what you don't like, and what behavior is bothering you, using any of these suggested responses or rewording a response that feels right for you.

   - "I don't like it when you…"
   - "It doesn't feel respectful when you.…"
   - "That looked and felt like harassment to me. Don't do that again."
   - "Don't go there. That crosses the line."
   - "What you just said felt really uncomfortable. I don't want you to say that to me again."
   - "You know, I would never say that to anyone. No one needs to hear that kind of stuff here at school."
   - "Look _____, you're my friend. And I've told you before, I don't like it when you say/do_____. It feels like you don't respect my feelings. Please stop using those words. Can you do that?"
   - "I feel disrespected/upset/uncomfortable when I hear you say that to me. I don't deserve hearing that and neither does anyone else."
   - "You know, earlier today, when you said_____, I really felt uncomfortable/disrespected. Please don't say that again."

3. Exit. You don't want to wait for a response or a miraculous conversion. Waiting for an apology or change of attitude risks escalating the situation. Leaving the scene, turning around, walking the other way, or focusing attention elsewhere is what you need to do.

If you're nervous about nonviolently confronting a person who is an aggressor or an instigator, that's a good indication that it's time to inform adults about the problem. "Exiting" can sometimes be a good option.

Responding to Bullying and Harassment: Guidelines for Allies

Many targets of harassment laugh at the beginning because they are nervous or embarrassed. They may believe or hope that they can just "laugh it off." Often aggressors and bystanders misinterpret the laughter, thinking it means the target doesn't mind.

Without allies, the cycle of harassment and bullying continues unchecked.

If you see someone being targeted, you might try responding in the following ways:

1. Say the aggressor's name and show respect.

2. Tell the aggressor to stop, name what you see, and why you don't like it:
   - "Knock it off with the abusive language, okay? No one deserves to hear that."
   - "I saw that and it looks like harassment to me. Lay off."
   - "If you had said that to me, I would have felt really uncomfortable/ disrespected. I don't want to hear that kind of stuff when I'm around."
   - "You know, if Mr._____ had heard that he would have labeled that remark as harassment. Clean up the language, OK?"
   - "That really sounds like a stereotype to me. I don't know _____ well enough to make that judgment."
   - "Where did that come from? We don't say stuff like that here. That's not what this school is about. Please don't say that here."
   - "I heard that. At this school, that's not OK to say to her/him, me, or anyone else."
   - "Hey, that's an ouch. I wouldn't want anyone to say that to me."
   - "Watch the language, huh? That's not OK to say to anyone."
   - "Look _____, you're my friend. And I've told you before, I don't like it when you say/do _____ around me. It feels like you don't respect my feelings. Please stop using those words. Can you do that?"
   - "You know, earlier today, I heard you say _____ to _____. If you had said that to me I would have really felt _____. Please don't say that to her/him or anyone else."

3. Take action:
   - Help the targeted person to leave the scene.
   - Go with the targeted person to report the incident.
   - Report the incident yourself.

Being an Ally

CASEL SEL Competencies

SO Social Awareness
SM Self-Management

■ Agenda

Gathering: Pair Share—Tell About a Time …

Agenda Review

Activity 1: Role Play Preparation

Activity 2: Role Play Presentation

Debriefing

Closing: Quote

■ Materials

Handout—Interrupting Harassment and Bullying: Guidelines for Allies

Handout—Role Play Scenarios

■ Prep

Place the Agenda on the board or on a chart

Make copies of the handout Interrupting Harassment and Bullying: Guidelines for Allies—one for each student.

If desired, chart the role-play guidelines and/or the goals of the role plays outlined in Activity 1, #3

Cut the Role-Play Scenarios handout into strips—one scenario per group

Gathering: Pair Share—Tell About a Time…

1. Group students into pairs (see the Teaching and Learning Strategies Appendix for suggestions on random pairing). Give pairs 3 minutes to discuss these questions:

   ⊙ Tell about a time when you saw an incident of harassment or bullying at school or in your neighborhood.

   ⊙ What did you do?

   ⊙ What, if anything, do you wish you had done differently?

2. Bring the class back together and debrief the activity with these questions:

   ⊙ How did it feel to be telling someone how you reacted in a situation like this? Was it easy or difficult? Why?

   ⊙ How did most people react in this situation?

   ⊙ What do people wish they had done differently?

Agenda Review

We have talked a great deal about the issues of harassment and bullying, what we can do to deal with these issues, and how to stand up against unfair treatment of ourselves and others. Today we're going to prepare and present some role plays in which we put our skills to the test. Our first Activity will be preparing a role play to present to the class, in order to show someone moving from being a bystander to becoming an ally during an incident of harassment or bullying. During the presentations of those role plays, in Activity 2, the class will identify effective ways to be an ally, in order for us to become more adept in that role.

Explain that the Debriefing will allow the class to create a list of those effective ways, and the Closing will ask us to reflect on a quote from a dark time in WWII.

Activity 1: Role Play Preparation

1. Distribute copies of the handout Interrupting Harassment and Bullying: Guidelines for Allies. Review the handout, and invite students to use the ideas in their role plays and to add any they think would be effective. Remind students that allies confront the situation nonviolently.

2. Divide the class into six groups and give each group one of the role play scenarios. (See the Teaching and Learning Strategies Appendix for suggestions on random grouping, or if you randomly paired for the Gathering, you might combine two pairs into a group.) In each scenario, the incident is reaching a crisis point where there will be a confrontation between the characters.

3. Each group should create a brief role play (3 minutes or less) that demonstrates what could happen in this confrontation if the ally helps the target and if the bystander has a change of heart and becomes an ally. The point of the role play is to show ways that allies and bystanders can stop harassment or bullying or ways that targets can stand up for themselves. In their role plays, groups should:
   - Briefly show what happens during the incident. This should be brief because the emphasis of the role play is on how to help the target, not on the harassment or bullying.
   - Show the target trying to confront the aggressor or the instigator.
   - Show the bystander watching the incident.
   - Show the ally helping in some way.
   - Show the bystander having a change of heart and starting to help.

Role-Play Guidelines

- You can name the characters and add other details, as long as they do not detract from the main message of how to end the harassment or bullying. Names may not be people you know.
- Do not use bad language or any real physical violence.
- Emphasize how to be a good ally in the role play. Do not emphasize the harassment or bullying. It might be more fun to role play that part, but it is more important that you demonstrate how to be a good ally.
- The role play will be stopped if the guidelines are not followed.

[**Cautionary Note:** Teachers or other adults should monitor the groups closely to make sure that students who are targets of harassment or bullying in real life are not forced to be targets in the role play. Teachers can assign the roles in each group if this is happening or is in danger of happening.]

"Love and compassion are necessities, not luxuries. Without them, humanity cannot survive."

—DALAI LAMA

Activity 2: Role Play Presentation

1. Give each group 3 minutes to present their role play to the large group. After each group's presentation, one of the group members should ask the large group these questions:

    ◉   What type of harassment or bullying did you see in our role play?

    ◉   What ally strategies did we demonstrate?

2. After all six groups have presented their role plays, briefly summarize the ally strategies demonstrated.

Debriefing

Ask:

◉   What did it feel like to act as an ally in the role plays?

◉   What did it feel like to be the target?

◉   How did it feel to have a change of heart as the bystander?

If groups have come up with additional effective comments, add them to the handout.

Closing: Quote

Read this famous quotation: "In Germany, they came first for the Communists, but I didn't speak up because I wasn't a Communist. Then they came for the Jews and I didn't speak up because I wasn't a Jew. Then they came for the trade unionists, but I didn't speak up because I wasn't a trade unionist. Then they came for the Catholics and I didn't speak up because I was a Protestant. Then they came for me—and by that time, no one was left to speak up." Martin Niemoller

Ask:

◉   What does this quote mean to you?

◉   How does it apply to being a good ally?

HANDOUT

Interrupting Harassment and Bullying: Guidelines for Allies

1. If you witness harassment, never enable the aggressor by laughing or stopping to just watch. Help the target by being a good ally. Speak up for him/her without putting anyone down. Try saying something like:
   - "Chill."
   - "Knock it off with the abusive language. No one deserves to hear that."
   - "I don't think that's funny."
   - "That's really cold—don't go there."
   - "Where did that come from? We don't say that kind of stuff here."
   - "That's just a rumor. Drop it."
   - "I saw that and it looked like harassment/bullying to me. Lay off."

OTHER THINGS ALLIES COULD SAY ...

_____

_____

_____

_____

2. When speaking to the person being harassed, say something like:
   - "I think they're being cruel."
   - "They're looking for trouble. This isn't worth it. Let's get out of here."
   - "You don't deserve this."

OTHER THINGS ALLIES COULD SAY ...

_____

_____

_____

_____

3. It is especially effective if two or more allies speak up, because it helps prevent the harasser or bully from turning on a single ally.

4. Take action. Help the target leave the scene. Go with the target to report the incident or report the incident yourself.

Role Play Scenarios

Role Play 1: *Interrupting Sexual Harassment*

The target and another student are study partners. They often hang out together after school to finish their homework. The aggressor and the instigator both secretly like the other student but don't have the courage to tell him/her so they take it out on the target. The instigator frequently tells the aggressor that he's heard that the target and the other student are messing around. This makes the aggressor really mad. The aggressor and the instigator confront the target on the bus after school.

Role Play 2: *Interrupting Class-Related Harassment*

One day at lunch, the target sat down at the same table as the aggressor and his friends. When they told her to move, she said, "Why? I don't have to." The aggressor is furious and starts a campaign, fueled by the instigator, to make the target pay for acting out of line. The aggressor frequently insults her (and her family) and makes fun of the way she's dressed, calling her "ghetto girl," "stinky," and "raggedy-dressed stray." The target is sitting by herself at lunch when the aggressor and the instigator confront her.

Role Play 3: *Interrupting Religious/Cultural Harassment*

The target wears a headscarf to school because her religion requires that males and females cover their heads. She is just learning English and thinks that's why she's being picked on. The aggressor has started knocking off her headscarf and calling her a religion freak. The situation is getting out of control because the instigator keeps spreading rumors about the target and teasing the aggressor for not fighting. The aggressor and the instigator confront the target in the hallway between classes.

Role Play 4: *Interrupting Ability-Level Harassment*

The target is in the aggressor's math and gym classes. The target sometimes gets nervous in math and gives the wrong answers during math team competitions and is just not very good in soccer, which is the sport they're playing in gym right now. The aggressor is very competitive and thinks that the target is holding them back in both math and gym. The instigator constantly rolls her eyes at the target and makes funny faces when he gives wrong answers. This really gets the math class laughing. The aggressor and the instigator confront the target in the locker room after the soccer team loses again.

Role Play 5: *Interrupting Body-Size-Related Harassment*

The target is trying out for the spirit team at school and has a pretty good shot at getting the last slot on the team. The target doesn't look like the others on the team, who are all small and agile. The aggressor and instigator snub the target at practice and call the target names trying to get him/her to quit. That way they can keep the team "pure." Just before the final tryouts, the aggressor and the instigator confront the target after practice.

Role Play 6: *Interrupting Homophobia-Related Harassment*

The target's mom is divorced and has a close relationship with her sisters and female friends. The instigator started a rumor that the target's mom is a lesbian and so therefore the target must be gay too. The aggressor left a note saying that on the target's desk. The aggressor and the instigator confront the target on the way home from school.

HANDOUT

GRADE 9
LESSONS ONE – SIX

Establishing a Safe, Respectful, and Supportive Classroom

Setting the Stage for Learning about Bullying and Harassment

CASEL SEL Competencies

SA Self-Awareness
RS Relationship Skills

■ Agenda

Gathering: Classroom Scavenger Hunt

Agenda Review

Activity: Class Guidelines

Debriefing

Closing: Easy and Hard

■ Materials

Handout—Classroom Scavenger Hunt

One piece of chart paper, if desired, for Activity

■ Prep

Place the Agenda on the board or on a chart

One copy of Classroom Scavenger Hunt handout for each student

Gathering: Classroom Scavenger Hunt

1. Give each student a copy of the Classroom Scavenger Hunt. Students have 10 minutes to interview other participants in search of individuals who fit the 24 categories listed. After they find a match for a particular category, they should write that person's name in the square. The goal of this activity is to interview as many people as possible; a name can appear only once on the sheet.

2. After 10 minutes, ask students to return to their seats. Choose several categories to discuss and ask students to raise their hands if they fit into that category. Ask them to do a demonstration in front of the group if appropriate.

Agenda Review

Discuss with students the positive aspects of having a classroom with such a diversity of experiences and opinions, and how that makes a classroom so much more interesting and stimulating. However, unless a classroom environment values differences and welcomes many opinions, this diversity can sometimes be challenging. One way to harness the energy of a group of people, and make it positive energy is to create some guidelines for working together.

Explain: As the Agenda shows, the Activity today will be to create a set of guidelines together, guidelines that will help us work well together, and will be particularly helpful as we begin to talk about the sensitive issues of harassment and bullying. The Debriefing will help us to look at our guidelines and think about how to keep them. We'll close with some thoughts about making the guidelines real.

Activity: Class Guidelines

1. Ask questions to help the group begin to think in term of guidelines. Chart their responses on chart paper, or on the board.

    Ask:

    ⊙ **How do we need to treat each other and speak to each other so that we can all feel valued and supported?**

    ⊙ **How can we show respect for each other?**

    ⊙ **What behavior will the group not accept?**

Offer examples if the group is having trouble coming up with ideas. Class Agreements usually include things like respect, talk one at a time, no side talking, okay to have different opinions, positive attitude, be supportive of others, etc. Feel comfortable restating the suggestions in positive terms, for example, "no side talking" might be changed to "one person speaks at time."

2. You might pause after suggestions that are broad in scope, and take a moment to be specific (for example, "What makes a good listener?" or "How does someone show 'respect'?" Many of these items are culturally linked and are not universally practiced in the same way). These specifics can be noted on an additional paper, listed on the board as you go, or taught as separate lessons (see the Recommended Resources Appendix for additional curricula).

3. After everyone has contributed, ask if there are any guidelines that can be combined because they are similar. Make sure that students understand that you are grouping similar ideas, not changing their words.

4. Once each suggestion has been refined into a guideline, ask students if they can agree to that guideline. Keep in mind that you are working to a consensus, so avoid a voting situation.

Debriefing

Read over the list of guidelines the class has created.

> Ask:
> ◉ **How do you think these guidelines will help our class be supportive and encouraging, and one in which we are safe to be who we are?**
> ◉ **Is there a way we can be gently reminded when we forget to adhere to the agreements?**

Students sometimes come up with harsh punishments because that is what they've heard elsewhere. Point out that it is helpful to practice kind ways to remind others about unfavorable behavior and to say things such as, "I don't like it when you say ___. We agreed that we would be respectful, and that doesn't feel respectful to me."

Closing: Easy and Hard

Ask students to respond to these questions, popcorn style (see the Teaching and Learning Strategies Appendix):

- ◉ What is something that will be easy for you to adhere to in the guidelines we just created?
- ◉ What is something that might be harder?

> *"The best way to understand people is to listen to them."*
>
> —RALPH NICHOLS

Classroom Scavenger Hunt
Find Someone Who …

HANDOUT

Has the same eye color as you do:	Can speak two languages:	Can cross their eyes: (requires a demo!)
Likes to sing in the bathroom:	Is the oldest of their siblings:	Can bench-press their own weight:
Has six or more people in their family:	Has a pet other than a dog or cat:	Had pizza for dinner this week:
Is the youngest in their family:	Can roll their tongue: (requires a demo!)	Plays a sport:
Plays an instrument or sings:	Is wearing red:	Can touch their head to their toes: (requires a demo!)
Likes to read:	Likes to play videogames:	Volunteers their time to help others:
Has traveled outside the United States:	Likes to babysit:	Likes to draw or paint:
Was born in the same month as you were:	Has braces:	Was born in a state other than the one we're in:

Identifying Bullying and Harassment

CASEL SEL Competencies

SA   Self-Awareness
SO   Social Awareness
RS   Relationship Skills

■ Agenda

Gathering: Go-Round—
    Something I'm Proud Of

Agenda Review

Activity 1: Concentric Circles—
    Our Experiences

Activity 2: Defining Bullying and
    Harassment

Debriefing

Closing: New Learning

■ Materials

Chart paper

■ Prep

Place the Agenda on the board
    or on a chart

Gathering: Go-Round—Something I'm Proud Of

In a go-round, ask students to respond to this question: Something I'm very proud of is ___. Begin the activity with your own contribution.

After everyone has contributed, challenge the students to try to remember another student's response. Allow only one answer per student (for example, "I remember that Jay said he was proudest of his math skills") and see if the class can remember everyone's responses.

Agenda Review

In today's Activities, we'll be exploring the definition of bullying and harassment. First, we'll talk about our experiences and opinions, and then we'll create a web of words to refine our definition of this issue. Explain that in the Debriefing students will be categorizing the examples into kinds of bullying and harassment, and in the Closing, they will be invited to share their thoughts on how the Activities might have opened them up to some new thoughts and insights.

Activity 1: Concentric Circles—Our Experiences

1. Divide the class into two equal groups (if you don't have an equal number, you may join one). One group forms a circle, and then faces outward. The second group forms a second circle around the first one, facing in. Each person in the inner circle faces a partner in the outer circle. (If you don't have enough room to make circles, parallel rows will work. This activity is more fully explained in the Teaching and Learning Strategies Appendix.)

2. Explain that you will be posing a question and then each person will have 1 - 2 minutes to share with their partner; all pairs will speak simultaneously. Identify whether the inside or outside person will speak first. After 1 - 2 minutes, you will signal that the other partner needs to begin to speak. When both partners have answered the first question, ask one of the circles to move two or three spaces to their right. Then pose the second question, and repeat the process. After that question, have the other circle move two places to their right, and so on.

Questions:
- Tell about a time when you saw an incident of harassment or bullying at school or in your neighborhood. Who was involved? What happened?
- Have you ever heard of anyone being bullied or harassed online or with the use of instant messaging or texting? What happened?
- Why do you think people bully or harass others?

3. Bring the class back together and ask for volunteers to answer each of the questions posed.

Activity 2: Defining Bullying and Harassment

1. Write the words "harassment" and "bullying" in the center of the board or on a piece of chart paper. Ask students what words or phrases come to mind when they see these two words. Add their contributed words to the board or chart paper with lines stemming out from the word in the center. You may choose to cluster like responses together. (See the Teaching and Learning Strategies Appendix for a more detailed description.)

2. Ask for volunteers to define harassment and bullying based on the ideas generated in the webbing. Write the definitions on the board. One definition might be: Harassment and bullying are any inappropriate, unwanted, or cruel behaviors that make someone feel uncomfortable, threatened, or embarrassed. You might also explain that bullying can be differentiated from harassment. Harassment is linked to aspects of one's identity, e.g., gender, race, sexual orientation, etc.

3. Point out that these are sometimes a single act, but more often are composed of repeated acts performed over time. The target (the person being harassed or bullied) and the aggressor (the person doing it) do not have to agree about what is happening. The aggressor might say, "I was just joking," but if the target feels threatened, then it's harassment or bullying. Aggressors can exert verbal, social, or physical power over a target.

4. If the topic does not arise from the discussion, explain to students that "cyber-bullying" is a term for acts such as these that occur using the Internet or other digital technologies. In the last few years, it has become as great a concern as traditional bullying, and perhaps greater according to some statistical data. According to the Fall 2010 issue of *Teaching Tolerance*, anywhere from one-third to one-half of youths have been targeted by cyber-bullies. Incidents of online bullying have led to documented incidents of "bullycide," students who take their own lives as a result of the torment from others.

5. Explain that students will have the opportunity to talk more about appropriate responses to bullying and harassment in later lessons.

"I'm not concerned with you liking or disliking me. All I ask is that you respect me as a human being,."

—Jackie Robinson

Debriefing

Explain: Now that we've created a definition for this kind of behavior, let's brainstorm some of the harassment and bullying you talked about in the first Activity, and categorize them into Verbal, Social, and Physical.

Chart students' responses. Possible responses might include:

Verbal
- name-calling
- threats
- comments on people's appearance
- sexual harassment (verbal)

Social
- exclusion
- humiliation
- rumors and gossip
- ignoring people
- mean tricks

Physical
- intimidation
- unwanted touching
- assault
- threatening gestures
- destroying property
- sexual harassment (physical)
- pushing

Closing: New Learning

In a go-round, ask each person to share the most valuable or surprising thing they learned about bullying or harassment in this lesson.

Roles in Bullying and Harassment

CASEL SEL Competencies

SA Self-Awareness
SO Social Awareness
RS Relationship Skills

■ Agenda

Gathering: Pairs—Personal Experiences

Agenda Review

Activity 1: Roles in Harassment and Bullying

Activity 2: Rotation Stations— Questioning Roles

Debriefing

Closing: Thinking About ___

■ Materials

Chart paper—one piece for each of five groups

Set of markers for each group

■ Prep

Place the Agenda on the board or on a chart

If desired, chart the Roles in Harassment and Bullying in Activity 1. These may be used again in another lesson

Write one question from Activity 2 on each of the five pieces of chart paper

Gathering: Pairs—Personal Experiences

Group students into pairs (see the Teaching and Learning Strategies Appendix for suggestions on random pairing). Give pairs 3 minutes to discuss these questions:

⊙ Have you ever been harassed or bullied? What happened?

⊙ How did you feel about it and how did it affect your life?

⊙ Did anyone come to your aid or support you?

Agenda Review

Bullying and harassment are not new. However, with the advent of technology it has been amplified, and now schools are responding to these issues as never before. Explain that this lesson will be examining the roles people play in harassment and bullying, and will begin to explore possible ways to deal with these issues. There is no one, perfect way to respond to any harassment or bullying; everyone needs to have a number of choices at their disposal.

The Debriefing will provide a time for reflection about a school-wide commitment, and the Closing will be a time to share a new thought or idea that you've had as a result of our work together.

Activity 1: Roles in Harassment and Bullying

1. Ask the class to brainstorm the different roles that people take in a harassment or bullying situation. List their responses on the board or on chart paper, and then compare them to the ones below:

⊙ **Target:** A person or group being harassed or bullied.

⊙ **Aggressor:** A person who taunts, threatens, humiliates, victimizes, or physically harms the target. Also known as a bully.

⊙ **Instigator:** A person who spreads rumors, gossip, or makes up things to encourage others to harass the target. Instigating can be done verbally, on the Internet, through instant messages, or through graffiti in public places.

⊙ **Bystander:** A person who either witnesses or knows the target is being harassed or bullied and does or says nothing. Bystanders may be adults or even a friend of the target.

⊙ **Ally:** A person who stands up for the target by befriending her or him nonviolently and by challenging the aggressor's attacks.

2. Discuss what it means to be an ally. Emphasize that an ally is peaceful and nonviolent. Point out examples of peaceful and nonviolent struggles, such as the Civil Rights Movement of the 1950s - 1960s, when white, Latino, Native American, and other individuals allied with the African American community as they sought civil rights. What were some of the methods these allies used to help correct a social injustice or wrongdoing? (Mention some examples such as nonviolent marches, boycotts, standing up for victims, and speaking out against Jim Crow laws.)

   ⊙ How do these examples apply to harassment and bullying in schools?

Activity 2: Rotation Stations—Questioning Roles

1. Divide the class into five groups. (See the Teaching and Learning Strategies Appendix for random grouping ideas, as well as a description of Rotation Stations.) Direct each group to stand at one of the areas you have designated. Give each group a piece of chart paper that has one of the following questions written on it:

   ⊙ What can *targets* do when they are being harassed or bullied? Where can they get help?

   ⊙ What kinds of consequences should there be for *aggressors* at school?

   ⊙ Why do people become *instigators*? What can you do to prevent people from instigating conflict and social drama?

   ⊙ How can *bystanders* become allies?

   ⊙ How can *allies* confront instigators and work to educate the school about bullying and harassment?

2. Allow 2 minutes or so for the groups to brainstorm responses to their questions and record them on the chart paper. At the end of the time, have all of the groups rotate to another station, leaving their chart paper behind. At their new stations, groups should take another two minutes or so to read the question(s) and add their responses to the list started by the previous group. Continue until all of the groups have comments on all of the stations, and have returned to their original question(s).

3. Ask volunteers from each group to read the question(s) and responses out loud to the class. Discuss the fact that most people play more than one of these roles every day. For example, a person may act as an ally in one circumstance but as an instigator when in a different crowd. (Note: If some of the responses are violent, remind students of the definition of an ally.)

4. Students also need to understand that there are legal ramifications to harassment. Should harassment be proved, there are often harsh consequences for the aggressors. The federal government has outlined the legal obligations each school has to protect students from student-on-student racial and national-origin harassment, sexual and gender-based harassment, and disability harassment. Many states have also established additional laws to protect students.

> *"One of the ill effects of cruelty is that it makes the bystanders cruel."*
>
> —THOMAS FOXWELL BUXTON

Debriefing

Explain that the purpose of categorizing what happens in a bullying or harassment situation helps to be able to understand the dynamics involved in people's relationships with each other. Some of the following lessons will continue to explore the choices we make in dealing with these situations. Ask the group:

- ⊚ What would it take to lessen the incidences of bullying and harassment school-wide?
- ⊚ What might be the benefit(s) to a school that decides to do this?

Closing: Thinking About …

Read the following sentence aloud, filling in the blank with your answer. In a Go-Round (see the Teaching and Learning Strategies Appendix) ask each group member to do the same. As we worked together, I kept thinking about _____.

Understanding Cliques

CASEL SEL Competencies

SO   Social Awareness
RS   Relationship Skills

■ **Agenda**

Gathering: Clique Opinion Continuum

Agenda Review

Activity 1: "Nasty Girls" by Alice Wong and Journals

Activity 2: Microlab on Cliques

Debriefing

Closing: New Awareness

■ **Materials**

Student journals or paper for journal writing

Signs: "Strongly Agree," "Not Sure," and "Strongly Disagree"

Masking tape (optional)

Timer

Handout—"Nasty Girls"

■ **Prep**

Place the Agenda on the board or on a chart

Create signs from construction paper—"Strongly Agree," "Not Sure," and "Strongly Disagree." If students are to read aloud for Activity 1, make copies of "Nasty Girls" by Alice Wong

If desired, chart the microlab questions for Activity 2

Gathering: Clique Opinion Continuum

1. Make a line with masking tape across the floor (or draw a line across the board). At one end place a Strongly Agree sign. Label the other end with a Strongly Disagree sign, and the middle Not Sure. (See the Teaching and Learning Strategies Appendix for a complete description of the Opinion Continuum.)

2. Explain that you will be asking students to position themselves along the line to show how they feel about some statements you will make. These statements have to do with the subject of the lesson, cliques. Cliques are groups that we belong to, which one dictionary defines as "a narrow exclusive circle or group of persons; one held together by common interests, views, or purposes."

3. Ask students to be as honest as possible in deciding where to stand, and let them know that when they have chosen a spot, they will be asked to privately speak with someone else who is there, explaining why they chose that spot.

   Statements:
   ⊙ I belong to a clique.
   ⊙ Belonging to a clique or group is important to me.
   ⊙ I find it uncomfortable to disagree with members of my clique or group, or with close friends.

4. After each statement, provide time for students to choose where to stand, and then give them a minute to explain to a partner nearby why they chose to stand there.

5. Thank students for their participation and have them resume their seats.

Agenda Review

Explain that this lesson will explore the issue of how and why young people belong to groups, and what impact group membership has on them.

We'll be reading "Nasty Girls," a story written by a high school student looking back at a junior high experience, and discuss its implications.

Explain that Activity 1 is an opportunity, again, for personal reflection, but this time in student journals. Activity 2 will be a group sharing called a Microlab. The Debriefing will be concerned with the outcomes that sometimes occur when people are in cliques and lose their identity. The Closing will be a sharing of new awareness this discussion has provided for us.

Activity 1: "Nasty Girls" and Journals

1. Read aloud "Nasty Girls" by Alice Wong (from *The Courage to Be Yourself: True Stories by Teens About Cliques, Conflicts, and Overcoming Peer Pressure*) or ask for volunteers to read several paragraphs. At the conclusion, ask for volunteers to summarize the story in two or three sentences.

2. Ask the class to respond in their journals to the following questions. (See the Teaching and Learning Strategies Appendix for a complete description of journal writing.) Read the first set of questions and have the class respond before reading the next.

   Questions:
   ⊚ Write about a time when you went against what people in a group thought or did. How did people react? How did you feel afterwards?
   ⊚ Write about a time you didn't go against the crowd but wished you had. What stopped you from speaking up at the time? What do you wish you'd done differently?

Activity 2: Microlab on Cliques

1. Divide the group into small groups of three. (See the Teaching and Learning Strategies Appendix for random grouping techniques. It also provides a more detailed description of the microlab format.)

2. Students will take turns responding to questions you will pose. Each person will have 60 seconds to respond to the question while the other two people listen carefully. Remind students that listening carefully means giving the speaker their full attention with no interrupting and no asking questions. Confidentiality is very important. Whatever is discussed in the microlab is to stay in the room. Students can decide how much information they want to share in the microlab. They do not need to disclose any information that would make them uncomfortable.

3. Groups should decide who will respond first. Read the first question, "Is it natural for people to form groups of friends or cliques? What are the benefits of belonging to a clique? How do cliques offer "social security,"? and allow 60 seconds for the first person to answer. Call time when 60 seconds is up and read the question again for the second person to answer, giving them 60 seconds. Do the same for the third person. Repeat this pattern for each of the other two questions.

   Additional questions for the microlab:
   ⊚ Why is it important to exclude others to maintain a clique's status?
   ⊚ Alice writes about how being in a clique made her "naive and closed-minded to new people." What are some other examples of how cliques hold people back or constrict a true sense of self?

"For me, being part of the popular group was okay, but it wasn't as important as being accepted by a group."

—ALICE WONG

Debriefing

After the final round, debrief the experience in a large group discussion. Read the following paragraph from "Nasty Girls": "I still feel guilty for the years I was a friend to those girls. Even though I didn't do most of the mean things they did, I continued to be part of their group."

Ask why they think Alice felt this way.

Explain that oftentimes bystanders to bullying feel guilty for not taking some action to defend those who are targeted. Say that in following lessons, the class will be exploring what other choices people who find themselves in Alice's situation can choose to take.

Closing: New Awareness

Ask the group why they think it can be so difficult to talk about the issues of cliques, exclusion, and other things that came up in this lesson during the discussions. Ask if there were new awarenesses from the day's discussion.

"Nasty Girls"

by Alice Wong

At the end of eighth grade, my classmates and I hung around after school signing each other's yearbooks. After my classmate Diana signed mine, I noticed she'd written, "Thank you for getting me into the gossip group."

I was shocked. I felt horrible. I didn't want people to associate me with a group labeled "the gossip group."

But the sad thing was, the girls in that gossipy group had been my closest friends for much of junior high. I don't know which I felt worse about—that I'd been part of their clique or that they'd kicked me out of it.

I met the members of my clique—Maggie, Marsha, Kayla, and Bethany—in sixth grade, the first year of junior high school. They were friendly and outgoing, and they helped me meet some new friends too—which I liked, since I was shy.

I was also naive and thought everyone was kind. I thought my new friends were funny. They talked to me about their problems and I confided in them. They seemed to fill all the qualities I was looking for in friends.

My friends were also striving to be popular, and as the semester progressed, they got what they wanted. People in school knew who they were. For me, being part of the popular group was okay, but it wasn't as important as being accepted by a group.

But during that year, I also began to notice changes in their personalities. They seemed to think that being popular meant putting everyone else down.

Kayla was the leader of the group. People wouldn't know whether or not the rest of us agreed with what she said because we were robots. We went along with her even if our own opinions were different.

One day, Kayla pointed at an eighth grader in the hall and commented loudly on "what a big nose" he had. The group laughed, but I didn't. I thought it was rude …

They loved to label people "dorky" or "geeky." They gossiped about how people acted or what they'd heard about them through friends.

I often thought about what would happen if I told them how I felt when they were mean, but I was afraid… I didn't want to lose their friendship… and thought it would be difficult to know a new group…

I was also afraid that if I spoke up, they'd all turn on me as well. I'd already had a taste of how it would feel to have their cruelty aimed at me.

Bethany had a particularly mean attitude and sometimes put me down like she did people outside the group. One day I was wearing a name-brand shirt and she came over to check the label.

"Is that real?" she said … as she peered and tugged on the back of my shirt.…My cheeks turned red in embarrassment.

She knew I wasn't the type who'd confront her, so she took advantage of my weakness. I felt hurt and angry that other members of the group did nothing to stick up for me.

When eighth grade began, I hung with the clique … but I also started to make new friends. I met people … in different classes and I could talk to them about things like our favorite bands and how we liked to sing and write poetry—things my old friends couldn't have cared less about …

Then one day, about three months before eighth grade ended, I sat down at my clique's usual lunch table.… After a few minutes, they came. Marsha and Maggie said hi, but Bethany and Kayla said nothing.

I didn't know why they were acting so distant toward me, but I thought that if I just left it alone, they'd get over whatever was bothering them. So I went to where some of my other friends were sitting and chatted with them for a while.

When I came back … Kayla gave me this stare. I knew something was very wrong indeed. She said she had something to discuss with Marsha and didn't want me to listen.…

I went to chat with my friend Jacqueline … but in the back of my mind I kept wondering what was up.…

The bell rang. On my way to the exit, Kayla called me over.… She told me she didn't like that I associated with friends outside the clique. She said that if I wanted to remain in the group, I had to follow their rules. She didn't exactly say that she wanted me out … but it was obvious from her expression that she did.

The rest of the group just stared silently at us.…Kayla snickered while she talked to me. She was having fun ejecting me.

I was shocked, and then, as her words sank in, it really started to hurt. I tried avoiding her. I felt like crying, but I didn't want to show her how badly her words hurt me.…

For weeks, I didn't have much of a social life. I kept to myself during school. I didn't hang with anyone after school. I wasn't up to doing anything fun.…

The way my friends turned on me made me feel like I couldn't trust anyone. I began analyzing everything the girls in the clique had said to me.… I was scared that if I were open with my new friends, they'd wind up hurting me too.

But, noticing I was blue, my new friends emailed me jokes and poems to lighten my mood.…

One Saturday, Eva and Melissa dragged me out to the park to play basketball and ride our bikes. Then we went out for lunch. I had so much fun. I began to realize who my true friends were.…

I realized I should have left the clique once I knew how they were, instead of waiting until they forced me out. I'm glad I'm no longer a part of that group. If I was, I might've become as closed-minded as they were and missed out on the opportunity to meet new people.

I still feel guilty for the years I was a friend to those girls. Even though I didn't do most of the mean things they did, I continued to be a part of their group.

… And when I went to high school, I was relieved to find that most people were much more respectful toward each other than in my junior high.

… Now I realize that being in a clique doesn't determine my worth. When I was in the clique, people in and out of the group saw me as naive, and I was closed-minded to new people. Now people see me as an outgoing, friendly, and kind person, which is a more accurate reflection of who I am and want to be.

"Nasty Girls" by Alice Wong is from *The Courage to Be Yourself: True Stories by Teens About Cliques, Conflicts, and Overcoming Peer Pressure*, used with permission from Free Spirit Publishing

Cyber-Bullying

CASEL SEL Competencies

SA Self-Awareness
SM Self-Management

■ Agenda

Gathering: Journal Response
Agenda Review
Activity 1: Pair-Share on Cyber-Bullying
Activity 2: Guidelines
Debriefing
Closing: New Learning

■ Materials

Student journals or materials for student writing

Chart on Roles in Bullying and Harassment used in a previous lesson

Chart paper—one piece per group of three

Markers

■ Prep

Place the Agenda on the board or on a chart

If desired, chart the questions for the Pair-Share in Activity 1

If desired, chart questions for creating Guidelines in Activity 2

Gathering: Journal Response

1. Write this quote by Nancy Willard on the board, or on chart paper, "When people use technology, there is a lack of tangible feedback about the consequences of their actions on others." Ask students to write for 3 or 4 minutes about what they think the quote means.

2. Ask the group to share, popcorn-style:
   - What do you think the quote by Nancy Willard means?

Agenda Review

Explain that the issue of cyber-bullying is something that was not even around just a few years ago. The advent of the personal computer led to an explosion in social networking, and with that came the same "people problems" that we've always faced, but with a new twist. Now, people can bully or harass others at a "safe distance." A common definition used for cyber-bullying is "when the Internet, cell phones or other devices are used to send or post text or images intended to hurt or embarrass another person."

Explain: For the Activities, we'll be getting a little more deeply into our experiences online and texting. Then, we'll be talking about how these issues affect our lives and coming up with some possible guidelines to ensure that people are treated fairly, even online.

Activity 1: Pair-Share on Cyber-Bullying

1. Group students into pairs (see the Teaching and Learning Strategies Appendix for suggestions on random pairing).

2. Students will take turns responding to questions about cyber-bullying. Explain that you will allow 3 minutes for each question, and extend the time if the class finds it necessary to complete their sharing.

3. Remind students that listening carefully means giving the speaker their full attention with no interrupting and no asking questions. Confidentiality is very important. Whatever is discussed in the pairs is to stay in the room. Students can decide how much information they want to share. They do not need to disclose any information that would make them uncomfortable.

Questions for the pair-sharing:
Have you ever had a miscommunication with someone online or while texting? Perhaps someone misinterpreted something you said, or "read

into" your comments something you did not intend to communicate. What happened?

How might the roles we discussed in the lesson about bullying and harassment translate to online experiences? These are:

- **Target:** A person or group being harassed or bullied.
- **Aggressor:** A person who taunts, threatens, humiliates, victimizes, or physically harms the target. Also known as a bully.
- **Instigator:** A person who spreads rumors or gossip, or makes up things to encourage others to harass the target.
- **Bystander:** A person who either witnesses or knows the target is being harassed or bullied and does or says nothing. Bystanders may be adults or even a friend of the target.
- **Ally:** A person who stands up for the target by befriending her or him nonviolently and by challenging the aggressor's attacks.

Talk about the consequences of cyber-bullying. Are they the same as "real time" situations? Could they be more complicated or drastic? In what way?

Activity 2: Guidelines

1. Have each pair of students join another pair, to create groups of four. Give each group a piece of chart paper and markers.

2. Ask each group to brainstorm some guidelines for dealing with cyber-bullying. Ask them to divide their brainstorming into three categories:
   - What to do if you are a target
   - What to do if you witness cyber-bullying
   - What might be the do's and don'ts in online (or phone) conduct—sometimes referred to as The Golden Rules of the Internet.

3. Provide at least 10 minutes for this activity, and signal when half of the time is up.

4. Ask each group to present their brainstormed ideas to the class.

Debriefing

After each group has presented their chart, debrief the experience in a large group discussion using the following questions:

- With regard to being the target of cyber-bullying, which suggestions seemed to you to be the most effective?
- What about witnessing the cyber-bullying?
- If we were to create our own Golden Rules of the Internet, which ones do you think are most important?

Closing: New Learning

Ask students to respond to these questions, popcorn-style (see the Teaching and Learning Strategies Appendix):

- Did anything surprise you in the discussions we had today?
- Is there any new learning you'll be taking away?

> *"Don't judge another man until you have walked two moons in his moccasins."*
>
> —NATIVE AMERICAN PROVERB

Becoming an Ally

CASEL SEL Competencies

SO Social Awareness
SM Self-Management

■ Agenda

Gathering: Back-to-Back Sharing
Agenda Review
Activity 1: Role Play Preparation
Activity 2: Role Play Presentation
Debriefing
Closing: Yarn Toss

■ Materials

Handout—Responding to
Bullying and Harassment:
Guidelines for Targets

Handout—Responding to
Bullying and Harassment:
Guidelines for Allies

Handout—Role Play Scenarios

■ Prep

Place the Agenda on the board
or on a chart

Make copies of the handout
Responding to Bullying and
Harassment: Guidelines for
Targets —one per student

Make copies of the handout
Responding to Bullying and
Harassment: Guidelines for
Allies —one per student

If desired, chart the role play
guidelines and/or the goals
of the role plays outlined in
Activity 1, #3

Make a copy of the handout
Role Play Scenarios, and cut
up so that each group only
receives one scenario

Gathering: Back-to-Back Sharing

1. Distribute the handouts—Responding to Bullying and Harassment:
    Guidelines for Targets and Responding to Bullying and Harassment:
    Guidelines for Allies. Discuss after students have read silently, or
    ask for volunteers to read sections. Ask for any comments. (Note: If
    students comment that some of the suggestions wouldn't work for them,
    acknowledge that everyone needs to feel comfortable with the choices
    they make in dealing with this difficult issue. However, with practice,
    more choices can become easier to use. Certainly if the environment
    values dealing with bullying and harassment, and refuses to ignore them,
    more people will feel comfortable in speaking up.)

2. Divide students into pairs (see the Teaching and Learning Strategies
    Appendix for suggestions on random pairing) and ask them to stand
    back-to-back. After each question you ask, students will turn to face
    each other and take turns answering the question. After both students
    have spoken, they will return to their back-to-back position. After each
    question, ask for a few volunteers to share their responses with the group.

    Questions:
    ⊙ What is one thing on the handouts that we discussed that you
      absolutely agree with?

    ⊙ What is one thing on the handouts that you would find hard to do?

    ⊙ Is there anything on the handouts that you think you could get better
      at with practice?

Agenda Review

Explain that the handouts you've been discussing can be helpful when
dealing with situations of bullying and harassment, but that it takes practice
to become better and more competent in managing bullying and harassment
situations.

Explain: Today will be an opportunity to practice. Our first Activity will be
preparing a role play to present to the class, showing someone moving from
being a bystander to becoming an ally during an incident of harassment or
bullying. During the presentations of those role plays, in Activity 2, the class will
identify effective ways to be an ally, to help us become more adept in that role.

Explain that the Debriefing will allow the class to create a list of those
effective ways, and the Closing will invite us to pledge actions in being an ally.

Activity 1: Role Play Preparation

1. Divide the class into six groups and give each group one of the role play scenarios. (See the Teaching and Learning Strategies Appendix for suggestions on random grouping, or if you randomly paired for the Gathering, you might combine two pairs into a group.)

2. Each group should create a brief role play (3 minutes or less) that demonstrates what could happen in this confrontation if an ally helps the target. Remind students to use the ideas from the handouts in their role plays and to add any they think would be effective. Remind students that allies confront the situation non-violently.

3. The point of the role play is to show ways that allies and bystanders can stop harassment or bullying. In their role plays, groups should:
    ⊚ Briefly show what happens during the incident. This should be brief because the emphasis of the role play is on how to help the target, not on the harassment or bullying.
    ⊚ Show the target trying to confront the aggressor or the instigator.
    ⊚ Show the bystander watching the incident.
    ⊚ Show the ally helping in some way.

Role Play Guidelines

  ⊚ You can name the characters and add other details, as long as they do not detract from the main message of how to end the harassment or bullying. Names may not be people you know.
  ⊚ Do not use bad language or any real physical violence.
  ⊚ Emphasize how to be a good ally in the role play. Do not emphasize the harassment or bullying. It might be more fun to role play that part, but it is more important that you demonstrate how to be a good ally.
  ⊚ The role play will be stopped if the guidelines are not followed.

[**Cautionary Note:** Teachers or other adults should monitor the groups closely to make sure that students who are targets of harassment or bullying in real life are not forced to be targets in the role play. Teachers can assign the roles in each group if this is happening or is in danger of happening.]

Activity 2: Role Play Presentation

1. Give each group 3 minutes to present their role play to the large group. After each group's presentation, one of the group members should ask the large group these questions:
    ⊚ What type of harassment or bullying did you see in our role play?
    ⊚ What ally strategies did we demonstrate?

2. After all six groups have presented their role plays, briefly summarize the ally strategies demonstrated.

> "Be kind whenever possible. It is always possible."
>
> —DALAI LAMA

Debriefing

Ask:

- ◉ What did it feel like to act as an ally in the role plays?
- ◉ What did it feel like to be the target?
- ◉ How did it feel to have a change of heart as the bystander?

If groups have come up with additional effective comments, add them to the handout.

Closing: Yarn Toss

Form a large circle. To start the activity, hold a ball of yarn, and say: To be a better ally, I will ___, and finish the sentence. Hold on to the end of the yarn, and toss the ball to someone across the circle, and ask that person to complete the same sentence. That person then tosses the ball to someone across the circle, while holding on to their part of the yarn. The next person should complete the sentence and pass the ball, and so on until everyone is holding a strand of yarn.

Responding to Bullying and Harassment: Guidelines for Targets

Ignoring isolated incidents may work, but a consistent problem of harassment will probably continue unless you act to stop it.

You might try to respond in the following ways:

1. Say the aggressor's name and show respect. Sometimes this means saying something like, "Steven, I don't mean any disrespect. I just want you to know.…"

2. Tell the aggressor what you don't like, and what behavior is bothering you, using any of these suggested responses or rewording a response that feels right for you.

   ⊙ "I don't like it when you _____."

   ⊙ "It doesn't feel respectful when you _____."

   ⊙ "That looked and felt like harassment to me. Don't do that again."

   ⊙ "Don't go there. That crosses the line."

   ⊙ "What you just said felt really uncomfortable. I don't want you to say that to me again."

   ⊙ "You know, I would never say that to anyone. No one needs to hear that kind of stuff here at school."

   ⊙ "Look _____, you're my friend. And I've told you before, I don't like it when you say/do _____. It feels like you don't respect my feelings. Please stop using those words. Can you do that?"

   ⊙ "I feel disrespected/upset/uncomfortable when I hear you say that to me. I don't deserve hearing that and neither does anyone else."

   ⊙ "You know, earlier today, when you said _____, I really felt uncomfortable/disrespected. Please don't say that again."

3. Exit. You don't want to wait for a response or a miraculous conversion. Waiting for an apology or change of attitude risks escalating the situation. Leaving the scene, turning around, walking the other way, or focusing attention elsewhere is what you need to do.

If you're nervous about nonviolently confronting a person who is an aggressor or an instigator, that's a good indication that it's time to inform adults about the problem. "Exiting" can sometimes be a good option.

HANDOUT

Responding to Bullying and Harassment: Guidelines for Allies

Many targets of harassment laugh at the beginning because they are nervous or embarrassed. They may believe or hope that they can just "laugh it off." Often aggressors and bystanders misinterpret the laughter, thinking it means the target doesn't mind.

Without allies, the cycle of harassment and bullying continues unchecked.

If you see someone being targeted, you might try responding in the following ways:

1. Say the aggressor's name and show respect.

2. Tell the aggressor to stop, name what you see, and why you don't like it:
   - "Knock it off with the abusive language, okay? No one deserves to hear that."
   - "I saw that and it looks like harassment to me. Lay off."
   - "If you had said that to me, I would have felt really uncomfortable/ disrespected. I don't want to hear that kind of stuff when I'm around."
   - "You know, if Mr. _____ had heard that he would have labeled that remark as harassment. Clean up the language, OK?"
   - "That really sounds like a stereotype to me. I don't know _____ well enough to make that judgment."
   - "Where did that come from? We don't say stuff like that here. That's not what this school is about. Please don't say that here."
   - "I heard that. At this school, that's not OK to say to her/him, me, or anyone else."
   - "Hey, that's an ouch. I wouldn't want anyone to say that to me."
   - "Watch the language, huh? That's not OK to say to anyone."
   - "Look _____, you're my friend. And I've told you before, I don't like it when you say/do _____ around me. It feels like you don't respect my feelings. Please stop using those words. Can you do that?"
   - "You know, earlier today, I heard you say _____ to _____. If you had said that to me I would have really felt _____. Please don't say that to her/him or anyone else."

3. Take action:
   - Help the targeted person to leave the scene.
   - Go with the targeted person to report the incident.
   - Report the incident yourself.

Role Play Scenarios

1. During gym class, one student shows that he or she is not skilled at the sport that is being played. The instigator talks to the aggressor a couple of times, pointing at the behavior. The aggressor begins to taunt the target.

2. During a passing period, the aggressor calls the target a name and uses some threatening language. It becomes clear that there is some history between the two and other students begin to notice and gather around.

3. In a classroom, students are taking turns reading aloud from the textbook. The target is making mistakes, and the instigator begins to nudge the aggressor to notice and do something. The aggressor makes nasty comments to the target.

4. All of the students are between classes, on a break, and in the hallways. The aggressor makes fun of the target's personal appearance, to the delight of the instigator, who has encouraged this behavior.

5. It is lunchtime, and the target approaches a lunch table where the instigator and the aggressor are sitting. The target begins to sit down, and the instigator says something to the aggressor, who speaks up about the target not being allowed to sit there.

6. A group of students are in the hallway, all talking about something they've read on Facebook the night before. The target approaches and everyone stops talking. The instigator begins to talk to the others about the postings that concern the target and something he/she is supposed to have done. The aggressor taunts the target about certain behaviors that are outlined in the posting.

GRADE 10
LESSONS ONE – SIX

Establishing a Safe, Respectful, and Supportive Environment

Setting the Stage for Learning about Bullying and Harassment

CASEL SEL Competencies

SA Self-Awareness
RS Relationship Skills

■ Agenda

Gathering: Respect

Agenda Review

Activity 1: Getting to the Heart of It

Activity 2: Group Agreements

Debriefing

Closing: Easy and Hard

■ Materials

2 heart-shaped pieces of construction paper

Handout—Line Cards

■ Prep

Place the Agenda on the board or on a chart

Cut out two identical heart shapes from the construction paper

Make one copy of the Line Cards handout, cut into lines

Chart paper labeled Group Agreements

Gathering: Respect

In a go-round (see the Teaching and Learning Strategies Appendix) ask students to share one thing that someone can do or say that shows respect.

Agenda Review

Explain that a classroom is an environment just like any other—one's home, or workplace, or a place where people congregate for social or physical activities. The intention of the lesson today is to explore ways that people interact in their environments, and recognize that a supportive and positive environment is usually more productive. In order to communicate openly and honestly, and to share opinions respectfully, it's helpful to establish guidelines for the classroom.

In the first Activity, we'll be telling a group story about a day in the life of a student. We'll be discussing the effect that the words people choose to say to him can have on this person. Our discussion will lead to our establishment of some guidelines—ones we can agree to in order to create a supportive and respectful environment in our classroom.

The Debriefing will be an opportunity to say how you might put these Guidelines into practice, and then the Closing will be a time for some personal sharing.

Activity 1: Getting to the Heart of It

1. Distribute the Line Cards #1 to #14 to various students. Make sure to pass them out in numerical order so that it is easy for students to read their cards in sequence. At certain points in the story, students will read their cards aloud.

2. Begin by holding up one of the hearts and explaining that every person starts out in life thinking that he or she is important—someone who thinks important thoughts, who has important feelings, someone who matters. This is called our self-concept. Ask students what is meant by self-concept and explore with them where we might get messages about our self-concept.

3. Begin telling the story below. When it is time for a student to read from his or her card, pause and look in that student's direction. After you hear each comment, tear off a piece of the heart. By the end of the story, there will be only a shred of heart left.

Jamal's alarm clock rings. He turns it off and sleeps another half hour. He gets up, gets into the shower, and hears his sister banging on the door.

She says, *Line Card #1*. ("Don't you know how to tell time? It's my turn in the bathroom!")

Jamal finishes in a rush and faces his sister at the door, who says, *Line Card #2*. ("You're such a slug. You were supposed to be out of here 15 minutes ago.")

He gets dressed, and heads for the kitchen. He sees his mother and says, "Hi, what's for breakfast?" His mother says, *Line Card #3*. ("Don't you know what time it is? I can't get your breakfast now. I have to leave in 10 minutes. There might be some cereal left, but good luck with that!")

Jamal's mother then looks at his wrinkled shirt and says, *Line Card #4*. ("That shirt looks awful. You're not going to wear that to school, are you?")

Jamal grabs his backpack and a banana and runs to get the bus. As he sits down, he remembers the English essay that he left on his desk. He worked on it late last night so that he could hand it in on time.

When he gets to school, Jamal tries to find his English teacher. He sees her in the copy room preoccupied with a stack of papers she's running through the copy machine. He starts to speak, but she cuts him off, saying, *Line Card #5*. ("Not now! Can't you see I'm busy?")

The bell rings, and he's now late for homeroom. He scrambles for his seat and accidentally knocks the books off the desk next to him. The student at the desk says, *Line Card #6*. ("Is it so hard to walk and watch where you're going at the same time? You're a jerk!")

His homeroom teacher looks up and says, *Line Card #7*. ("What is it this time? You're late again, you know.")

And so the day goes. In geometry class students are working in groups on proofs—not Jamal's favorite thing. He sits staring silently at the problem and one of his partners says, *Line Card #8*. ("So are you in this group or not? Don't you have anything to say?")

Between classes, Jamal sees his girlfriend. He calls out to her in the hall. He was so busy finishing his essay last night that he didn't text or call her, even though he said he would. She sees him and says, *Line Card #9*. ("Don't even think about an excuse! Leave me alone!")

When he gets to his English class, there's no time to talk with his teacher privately. At the end of class, when it's time to turn in his essay, his teacher notices he isn't turning it in and says, *Line Card #10*. ("So where's your essay, Jamal? Did the dog eat it again?")

At lunch Jamal sees his girlfriend in the cafeteria. She's with a bunch of her friends, and he asks if she has a minute to talk. She replies, *Line Card #11*. ("So now you want to talk! Wait until you read what I posted on Facebook when you didn't text last night!")

He walks away. A couple of his friends notice what's happened and give him a hard time. One of them says, *Line Card #12*. ("Guess you're not the big man anymore.")

Finally it's time for basketball practice. He's practicing free throws, and nothing is going in. The coach notices and says, *Line Card #13*. ("You've lost your touch. Take a walk and let someone else shoot.")

Jamal gets home. It's his turn to cook dinner, but all he wants to do is to sprawl on the couch, turn on some music, and turn off the day. He hears the door close as he opens his eyes. His mother walks into the living room and says, *Line Card #14*. ("Is this your idea of making dinner? I can't leave you in charge of anything.")

4. Discuss how negative comments make people feel. Ask what the opposite of a put-down is (affirmative statements, positive or encouraging words). Explain that supportive comments show respect, acceptance, and encouragement.

5. Hold up the other heart. Tell the same story again, but this time, ask students to suggest supportive, encouraging comments that could be said in place of the put-downs or negative ones we heard in the first story. This time the heart stays intact.

Activity 2: Group Agreements

1. Explain: Now that we've had a chance to explore this topic, we'll use this information to create some Group Agreements to ensure that positive and supportive comments and behaviors become a part of our classroom.

2. Label a piece of chart paper "Group Agreements." Ask questions like these to help the group begin to think in term of guidelines: How do we need to treat each other and speak to each other so that we can all feel valued and supported? How can we show respect for each other? What behavior would not be acceptable to our group? Have the group contribute specific agreements they would like to see adopted in the class so you can chart them on the paper. Offer examples if the group is having trouble coming up with ideas. Group agreements usually include things like respect, talk one at a time, no side talking, okay to have different opinions, positive attitude, be supportive of others, etc. Feel comfortable restating the suggestions in positive terms, for example, "no side talking" might be changed to "one person speaks at time."

3. You might pause after suggestions that are broad in scope, and take a moment to be specific (such as "What makes a good listener?" or "How does someone show respect?". Many of these items are culturally linked, and are not universally practiced in the same way).

4. After everyone has contributed, ask if there are any Agreements that can be combined because they are similar. Make sure that students understand that you are grouping similar ideas, not changing their words.

5. Once each suggestion has been refined into an Agreement, ask students if they can agree to that guideline. Keep in mind that you are working to a consensus, so avoid a voting situation.

Debriefing

Read over the list of Agreements the class has created.

Ask:
◉ How do you think these Agreements will help our class be supportive and encouraging?

◉ Is there a way we can be gently reminded when we forget to adhere to the Agreements?

Students sometimes come up with harsh punishment because that is what they've heard elsewhere. Point out that it is helpful to practice kind ways to remind others about unfavorable behavior and to say things such as, "I don't like it when you say ___. We agreed that we would be respectful, and that doesn't feel respectful to me."

Closing: Easy and Hard

Ask students to respond to these questions, popcorn style (see the Teaching and Learning Strategies Appendix):

- What is something that will be easy for you to adhere to in the Agreements we just created?
- What is something that might be harder?

A supportive and positive environment is usually more productive.

HANDOUT

Line Cards

1. "Don't you know how to tell time? It's my turn in the bathroom!"

2. "You're such a slug. You were supposed to be out of here 15 minutes ago."

3. "Don't you know what time it is? I can't get your breakfast now. I have to leave in 10 minutes. There might be some cereal left, but good luck with that!"

4. "That shirt looks awful. You're not going to wear that to school, are you?"

5. "Not now! Can't you see I'm busy?"

6. "Is it so hard to walk and watch where you're going at the same time? You're a jerk!"

7. "What is it this time? You're late again, you know."

8. "So are you in this group or not? Don't you have anything to say?"

9. "Don't even think about an excuse! Leave me alone!"

10. "So where's your essay, Jamal? Did the dog eat it again?"

11. "So now you want to talk! Wait until you read what I posted on Facebook when you didn't text last night!"

12. "Guess you're not the big man anymore."

13. "You've lost your touch. Take a walk and let someone else shoot."

14. "Is this your idea of making dinner? I can't leave you in charge of anything."

Defining Bullying and Harassment

CASEL SEL Competencies

SA Self-Awareness
RS Relationship Skills

■ Agenda

Gathering: Opinion Poll

Agenda Review

Activity 1: Defining Bullying and Harassment

Activity 2: Story—Examples of Harassment and Bullying

Debriefing: Pair Share—Tell About a Time …

Closing: Now I Know

■ Materials

Signs labeled "Sometimes," "Always," "Never"

Handout—Harassment Led to Suspensions at Smartville High School

Handout—Types of Harassment and Bullying

■ Prep

Place the Agenda on the board or on a chart

Create three signs labeled "Sometimes," "Always," "Never"

Make copies of Harassment Led to Suspensions at Smartville High School—one per student

Make copies of Types of Harassment and Bullying— one per student

Gathering: Opinion Poll

1. Post signs labeled, "Sometimes," "Always," and "Never" in different places around the room. Explain that when a statement describing a particular behavior is read, students should decide if the behavior is sometimes, always, or never harassment or bullying. Students should stand under the sign that reflects their opinion about the statement.

Are the following behaviors sometimes, always, or never harassment or bullying?

- ◉ Comments on one's body, dress, or personal appearance
- ◉ Casual physical contact like hugging, patting, or holding hands
- ◉ Graffiti in the bathroom
- ◉ Invitations for dates
- ◉ Initiation into sports teams
- ◉ Rumors
- ◉ Unflattering comments made online

2. After each round, ask several students standing under each sign to share their opinions about the statement. As students share, point out that it is the person being targeted who defines the action as bullying or harassment. In a different context or from a different person, it might not be considered harassment or bullying.

Agenda Review

Explain that the lesson today will begin to explore the sensitive issues of harassment and bullying. These issues can be difficult to discuss, and it will require that students remember the Class Agreements that they made in the previous lesson. Just as the Gathering demonstrated, what feels like harassment or bullying to one person, may not be seen as that by another. That fact, however, doesn't change the situation, and by talking about the issues, it is hoped that students will begin to recognize how important the issue has become in our society. Although bullying has always been a part of the human experience, modern inventions have enabled the effects of bullying and harassment to be intensified. Many studies have documented the negative effects of harassment and bullying, not only on the target of the action, but on the aggressor as well, and even those only involved as bystanders.

In the first Activity, we will attempt to reach a definition of harassment and bullying. The second Activity will move us more deeply into some examples and categories. In the Debriefing, we'll discuss some personal experiences of harassment or bullying, and then in the Closing, share any new awarenesses we've had a result of today's discussion.

Activity 1: Defining Bullying and Harassment

1. Write the words "harassment" and "bullying" in the center of the board or on a piece of chart paper. Ask students what words or phrases come to mind when they see these two words. Add their contributed words to the board or chart paper with lines stemming out from the word in the center. You may choose to cluster like responses together. (See the Teaching and Learning Strategies Appendix for a more detailed description of webbing.)

2. Ask for volunteers to define harassment and bullying based on the ideas generated in the webbing. Write the definitions on the board. One definition might be: Harassment and bullying are any inappropriate, unwanted, or cruel behaviors that make someone feel uncomfortable, threatened, or embarrassed. You might also explain that bullying can be differentiated from harassment. Harassment is linked to aspects of one's identity, e.g., gender, race, sexual orientation, etc.

3. Point out that these are sometimes a single act, but more often are composed of repeated acts performed over time. The target (the person being harassed or bullied) and the aggressor (the person doing it) do not have to agree about what is happening. The aggressor might say, "I was just joking," but if the target feels threatened, then it's harassment or bullying. Aggressors can exert verbal, social, or physical power over a target.

4. If the topic does not arise from the discussion, explain to students that "cyber-bullying" is a term for acts such as these that occur using the Internet or other digital technologies. In the last few years, it has become as great a concern as traditional bullying, and perhaps greater according to some statistical data. According to *Teaching Tolerance*, anywhere from one-third to one-half of youths have been targeted by cyber-bullies (Fall 2010). Incidents of online bullying have led to documented incidents of "bullycide," students who take their own lives as a result of the torment from others.

5. Students also need to understand that there are legal ramifications to harassment. Should harassment be proved, there are often harsh consequences for the aggressors. The federal government has outlined the legal obligations each school has to protect students from student-on-student racial and national-origin harassment, sexual and gender-based harassment, and disability harassment. Many states have also established additional laws to protect students.

Activity 2: Story—Examples of Harassment and Bullying

1. Read the newspaper article "Harassment Led to Suspensions at Smartville High School" aloud or ask for volunteers to read paragraphs. Ask the students to listen for behaviors in the article that could be considered harassment or bullying.

2. Discuss the examples the students heard in the article. Explain that harassment or bullying is about having power over someone else. Aggressors may exert physical, verbal, or psychological power over the target.

> *"Cruelty, like every other vice, requires no motive outside of itself; it only requires opportunity."*
>
> —GEORGE ELIOT

3. Write three list headings on the board or on chart paper: **Verbal, Social, Physical.** Ask students to categorize the examples heard in the article into the three headings. Some examples might include:

Physical
- Threatening gestures
- Destroying property
- Pushing
- Unwanted touching
- Weapons

Verbal
- Name calling
- Put downs
- Threats
- Obscene phone calls

Social
- Excluding
- Rumors/Gossip
- Ignoring
- Humiliation
- Mean tricks

4. Ask students to identify the five most common forms of harassment at their school. Place an asterisk next to these on the list.

5. Ask students why the boy in the article was the target of harassment or bullying. Why did the 11th graders choose him? This harassment/ bullying was based on age (the target was a 9th grader), but there are many types of harassment and bullying. Ask the group to name a few other types of harassment or bullying they have seen at their school (sexism, racism, etc.).

6. Distribute Types of Harassment and Bullying and read and discuss.

Debriefing: Pair Share—Tell About a Time …

1. Group students into pairs (see the Teaching and Learning Strategies Appendix for suggestions on random pairing). Give pairs 3 minutes to discuss a time when they saw an incident of harassment or bullying at school or in their neighborhood. Ask: What happened? What did you do?

2. Bring the class back together and ask for a few volunteers to relate their stories. Explain that in further lessons, there will be an opportunity to look more deeply into these issues. There will also be more information about dealing with these important issues.

Closing: Now I Know

Place the following sentences on the board and ask for volunteers to complete them: Before this discussion, I didn't know _____. After this discussion, I know _____.

Harassment Led to Suspensions at Smartville High School

By Susie Que

Smartville Daily News

Smartville, USA Many people think back to high school as the best years of their life. Not so for some students at Smartville High School, certainly not for one 9th grade boy who was the target of a recent harassment incident. The four students who instigated the incident were suspended on Friday.

The Smartville High School principal, Marianna Greenwood, declined to describe exactly what happened, but one of the students who observed the incident said that it began when several 11th graders "canned" a 9th grade student. "Those guys said that 9th graders are trash so they picked up a short 9th grader and put him in one of those big garbage cans in the hallway. Lots of students stopped to watch and laugh. I felt so bad for the kid. The guys started pushing and shoving him when he tried to get out."

Ms. Greenwood stated that administration learned of the incident from someone other than the students directly involved. One of the students who observed the incident quickly reported it to the office.

The incident occurred outside of Jack Connell's classroom. "I heard all this laughing and when I went out to the hallway, I saw what was going on. I thought they were just joking. After all, boys will be boys. I should know. I did some of the same things in high school."

Ramon Perez, the discipline principal, reported that the suspended students had a history of being disciplined for harassment offences against the targeted student. "We take harassment very seriously here so the suspensions are for three days. Students have to understand that there are consequences for their actions."

One of the target's friends, who asked to remain anonymous, said that this kind of harassment had occurred before. "We told him that if he just ignored the harassment it would go away. But I guess it didn't. It got worse." He explained that the suspended students had frequently called his friend names, thrown spitballs at him between classes, and written things about him in the boys' locker room.

The girl who reported the incident said she was tired of all the harassment and bullying at the school. "I was the target of vicious rumors when I was in 10th grade so I know how being the target of harassment feels. I had to do something. I'm going to talk to the kid at lunch and make sure he's okay."

Ms. Greenwood restated that any form of harassment is against school district policy. "Hopefully this will be a wake-up call for students and staff."

Types of Harassment and Bullying

- **Sexual harassment** is unwanted, unwelcome sexual comments or actions that include touching, gestures, sex-based insults, the spreading of sexually-oriented rumors, persisting in giving unwanted compliments, or making comments or actions which target an individual or group and/or make spectators uncomfortable. Sexually harassing comments can be spoken or written, using graffiti, slams, pagers, cell phones, or the Internet.

- **Racial harassment or bullying** includes racist comments and attacks on someone's skin color, ethnicity, native language, or national origin.

- **Gender-related harassment or bullying,** also called homophobic harassment or bullying, includes attacks on persons who are gay, bisexual, lesbian, or transgendered because of their real or perceived gender orientation. Examples include calling someone a "fag," a "lesbo," or calling someone you don't like "gay" or "queer."

- **Religious harassment or bullying** includes attacks on someone's religious beliefs, practices, or affiliation.

- **Size-based harassment or bullying** means taunting someone because of his or her height or weight.

- **Ability-level harassment or bullying** includes insulting a person because of a real or assumed physical or mental ability or disability. Examples include habitually calling someone "retard," "dummy," "nerd," or "geek" or making fun of individuals who use crutches, a hearing aid, glasses, or are academically above average.

- **Harassment or bullying based on class** includes teasing or ridiculing someone based on the amount of money or possessions they have or don't have.

- **Harassment or bullying based on looks** may include calling someone "UGG-ly" or referring to a female as a "dog."

Roles in Harassment and Bullying

CASEL SEL Competencies

SA Self-Awareness
RS Relationship Skills

■ Agenda

Gathering: Concentric Circles—Types and Effects of Harassment

Agenda Review

Activity 1: Roles in Harassment and Bullying

Activity 2: Opinion Continuum—Harassment and Bullying Roles

Debriefing

Closing: Go-Round

■ Materials

Handout—Journal Entry

Chart paper for roles

Signs labeled "Bystander," "Aggressor," "Ally," "Instigator," and "Target"

Handout—Role Cards

■ Prep

Place the Agenda on the board or on a chart

Chart the definitions of the roles in Bullying and Harassment (Activity 1 - #4)

Make signs labeled "Bystander," "Aggressor," "Ally," "Instigator," and "Target"

Make a copy of the Role Cards handout, and cut into strips

Gathering: Concentric Circles—Types and Effects of Harassment

1. Have students stand in a large circle. Count off by two's. Two's should step inside the circle and turn to face a one to form a pair. This sets up two circles, one inside of the other. If there is not a large open space in the room for a circle, modify the activity using rows of students instead of a circle. (See the Teaching and Learning Strategies Appendix for a more detailed description of Concentric Circles.)

2. Read the first two paragraphs of the "Journal Entry," which was written by the boy who was the target of harassment in the newspaper article in the previous lesson. Give pairs 1 minute to discuss the following questions and then ask several pairs to share their ideas.

    ◉ What examples of harassing behavior do you see in the boy's journal entry (name-calling, etc.)?

    ◉ What types of harassment did the boy mention (racism, sexism, etc.)? Label each type of harassment as it occurs in the journal entry.

3. After a brief large group discussion, the outside circle should move two places to the left. Read the next paragraph of the journal entry. Again, give the pairs 1 minute to discuss the above questions and then share their answers with the large group.

4. Repeat this process for each paragraph in the journal entry. Alternate between the inside and outside circle moving two places to the left.

5. After the group has been reseated, ask the following questions. Record the students' ideas on chart paper.

    ◉ How did the harassment and bullying affect the boy writing the journal entry? What are some other ways harassment and bullying could affect the target?

    ◉ How does harassment and bullying affect the school community?

Agenda Review

In the last lesson, we defined harassment and bullying and created some categories to talk about them. Today, we'll review a little and then explore the roles that are a part of most incidences.

Explain that the class will again use the Smartville High School story to look at the different roles involved in harassment or bullying in Activity 1. In the second Activity, students will then "become" some of the characters involved, and will be deciding what role was taken by their character.

The Debriefing will ask students to think about why it might be important to identify the roles in bullying and then in the Closing, students will share what may have been new information or information that will be of value to them.

Activity 1: Roles in Harassment and Bullying

1. To review the information from the last session, ask the following questions:
   - What is the definition of harassment and bullying?
   - What are some examples of harassing and bullying behavior (pushing, name-calling, etc.)?
   - What are the different types of harassment (based on race, gender, age, etc)?

2. Post the brainstorming ideas from the last session.

3. Read the newspaper article "Harassment Led to Suspensions at Smartville High School" again. Instruct the students to pay attention to how each character in the story responded to the harassment incident. Have students notice what each person did or said and try to determine how each person felt about the incident.

4. Ask the group to describe the different ways the characters responded in the article. Post the definitions of each role in harassment and bullying situations and discuss them using the article for examples.
   - **Target:** This is the person or group that is being harassed.
   - Aggressor: Also known as a bully, this person actively and repeatedly engages in behavior meant to taunt, threaten, humiliate, victimize, or physically harm the target.
   - **Instigator:** He/she spreads rumors or gossip, or makes up things to get the target in trouble. The instigator may use taunts or rumors to try to make the aggressor mad enough to harass the target. Instigating can be done verbally, in email or Internet chat rooms, or through graffiti in public places such as bathrooms, etc. Not all bullying and harassment has an instigator. Sometimes the aggressor is responsible for these actions.
   - **Bystander:** A person who stands by, witnesses, or knows that the target is being harassed or bullied and does or says nothing. Sometimes bystanders think that doing nothing will prevent them from being harassed or bullied themselves, or that it is "not their business." Bystanders can be both adults and students.
   - **Ally:** A person who stands up for the target by defending him/her nonviolently and by challenging the aggressor's attacks.

"If we have no peace, it is because we have forgotten that we belong to each other"

—MOTHER THERESA

5. Discuss what it means to be an ally. An ally stands up for the person being harassed or bullied, using strategies that do not escalate the situation, but are peaceful and nonviolent (i.e., without hitting, shoving, kicking, fighting, shouting, calling names, or putting down the other person, etc.).

An example of peaceful and nonviolent struggle is in the Civil Rights Movement of the 1950s - 1960s, when white, Latino, Native American, and other individuals allied with the African American community as they sought civil rights. These allies engaged in nonviolent means to help correct a social injustice or wrong that affected individuals as well as groups. What were some of the methods these allies used? Mention marches, boycotts, standing up for victims, speaking out against Jim Crow laws, etc. Ask students how examples like this apply to the issue of harassment and bullying in schools.

Activity 2: Opinion Continuum—Harassment and Bullying Roles

1. Post signs labeled "Bystander," "Aggressor," "Ally," "Instigator," and "Target" in different areas of the room. Explain to the group that each person will receive a role card that describes a person involved in the incident at Smartville.

2. Distribute a strip from the Role Cards to each student. Students should read the descriptions carefully and decide if their person is a target, aggressor, instigator, bystander, or ally. They should then go stand under that sign.

3. When everyone is standing under a sign, ask several people from each group to read their card and explain why they are standing under that sign.

Debriefing

1. While students are still standing under a sign, explain that in follow-up lessons, there will be time to explore what works to "interrupt" or intervene in harassment and bullying situations, both for the target and for the bystander who decides to become an ally.

2. Ask the class to respond to these questions, by speaking with a partner in their group:
   ⊙ In what ways might it help to identify the roles people take in harassment and bullying? (We might recognize our actions in naming them and realize how we are contributing to bullying and harassment situations.)
   ⊙ Think back to an incident you have witnessed at school. What role did you play?

Closing: Go-Round

In a go-round, ask each person to share the most valuable or surprising thing they learned about harassment and bullying in this lesson.

Journal Entry
October 21

I just can't believe how things have changed in the last few months! When my family moved here in July, I really thought it was going to be great starting at the high school. I mean, I'd been looking forward to starting high school ever since I finished eighth grade. Boy, was I wrong!

Like yesterday when these 11th grade guys passed me in the hallway they said 9th graders are trash. They picked me up and stuffed me in one of those big garbage cans in the hallway. When I tried to get out, they kept pushing me back in. All these kids just stood around watching and laughing. I was so embarrassed!! Things like this have happened before but my friends just said to ignore it and it would go away. Yah, right!

My sister gets crap all the time too. She's a senior and because she's the new girl at school, gets asked out a lot by some of the popular guys. She keeps saying "no," but they still ask and even make rude gestures at her. She told me that one guy even sneered, "What are you a lesbian or something?"

Gym class is the worst! Last week the coach told the captains to pick teams for basketball. The captains picked the better players, saying they didn't want me on their team because I couldn't pass and was too short to score. They said I would make a better basketball than a player. My sister feels bad for the overweight girls in her gym class because they're called "blimps" and no one wants them on their teams either. In the locker room, I saw some guys trip one of the Muslim kids and whisper, "What are you, some sort of religious nut? We don't want your kind here". You wouldn't believe the graffiti in there! The locker room is definitely not a place I like hanging around!

I'm just glad my family has some money. I mean it's bad enough for me already, but I heard these rich girls calling this one girl "ghetto girl" and "Ms. Payless" just because she doesn't wear expensive, cool clothes like they do. They got up and moved away when she sat down at their lunch table. I bet they're the ones who started all the rumors about her.

I guess I thought high school was going to be different. My other sister is in elementary school and gets called "retard" all the time, but I thought people would have grown up or something in high school. I hate coming to school and my grades are dropping so my parents are on my case too. Man, I'd like to get those guys back and show them how it feels!!!!!

ROLE CARDS

(for Activity 2: Opinion Continuum—Harassment and Bullying Roles)

HANDOUT

Target

I play on a sports team at Smartville High School. At the beginning of the season, some of my teammates taped my ankles and wrists together and then shoved me into the girls' locker room. They said it was just part of initiation but it really humiliated me.

I'm a junior at Smartville High School. Almost every day on my way to 6th period these seniors make really obscene gestures at me and pretend to grab my butt. I've tried going to class another way, but I can't make it to class on time without going down that hallway.

I'm an assistant coach for one of the sports teams at another high school in Smartville. When I just mentioned the word "harassment" at a coaches' meeting, the other coaches called me a "wimp" and said that maybe I should stop coaching if I didn't like what was going on.

I was glad to hear that those guys got suspended. The kids in my neighborhood are always making fun of me just because I use crutches. I wish someone would suspend them. I don't understand why they do it. Harassment and bullying is just plain cruel.

Aggressor

HANDOUT

Yah, I'll admit it. I put the kid in the trashcan. Suspending me was going way overboard though. Stuff like that is just part of being initiated into school. What's the big deal?

I pushed the kid when he tried to get out of the trashcan. Everyone in the hallway was laughing and it made them laugh even harder when he couldn't get out.

I don't see why they wrote that newspaper article. We do stuff like that all the time to new players on my sports team. We don't seriously hurt them; just give them a hard time is all. A little tape around the ankles never hurt anyone.

Smartville High School is getting overrun by foreigners. My friends and I want them to get the message loud and clear that they should go back to their own countries so we "accidentally" trip them in the hallway and play mean tricks on them.

I can't stand those stuck-up big shots who think they rule the school just because they have money. Sometimes I like to rough them up a bit just to show them who really owns the school.

One of my assistant coaches was concerned that harassment and bullying was happening to new players. Who does he think he is? I told him that there are plenty of other faculty members who could help coach if he wasn't comfortable with the team policies.

There's this kid on the bus who is so clumsy and stupid that he trips over everything. I can't help it if he trips over my feet when I stick them in the aisle. And those spitballs just seem to leap out of my hands at him. He must be a spitball magnet or something.

HANDOUT

Instigator

I'm friends with the guy who canned that 9th grader. He told me what he was thinking about doing and it sounded fun so I said, "That'll make for some good entertainment. Do it in the hallway so we can have a good seat for the show."

There's this boy in my lunch period. Sure, he's only in 10th grade and I'm a senior but he's so cute that I asked him out. I was furious when he said "no," so I told some of my guy friends how he disrespected me and they taught him a lesson after school.

My best friend was the one who put that boy in the garbage can. I shouted, "Extra points if you score a basket with the geek." Everyone laughed really hard at that so I kept shouting.

My boyfriend was the one who "canned" the 9th grader. I had told him that boy asked me out on a date. It wasn't exactly true, but it was kind of fun to see how my boyfriend reacted.

This girl in my history class thinks she's so great just because she's getting an "A." I couldn't take her superiority complex anymore yesterday so I wrote in the girls' bathroom that she slept around to get the "A."

My older brother is in college but his girlfriend is still in high school. I email him every night to tell him who his girlfriend has been talking to that day. It makes him really angry when she talks to other guys.

Bystander

I saw that kid get pushed and just kept going because it wasn't my business. I went through that kind of stuff last year when I was in 9th grade. I didn't want to get involved.

I saw the incident happen, and it was so funny that I just couldn't help laughing. They didn't really hurt the kid or anything.

My son is one of the students who got suspended. I think the school stepped way out of bounds in suspending him. This is just the kind of thing boys do. They were joking.

Those guys who got suspended are my friends. I knew what they were planning on doing, but how could I stop them? I mean, they'd be mad at me if I told them not to do it, and what's the big deal anyway? It's just part of being in 9th grade.

I'm a science teacher at Smartville High School. I heard some kids bragging about the incident in my third period class. They were laughing and causing quite a commotion, but it didn't have to do with science so it wasn't my business.

I go to the other high school in Smartville, and I see stuff like that happen all the time at our school. Some kids are just weak. They can't take it. Too bad for them.

HANDOUT

HANDOUT

Ally

I'm the school custodian and I saw what happened. I've seen it happen before and I'm tired of it. I put down my mop and yelled at the group, "You cut that out—I saw you and am reporting you for this."

I saw the whole thing happen. I went over and helped the boy get out of the garbage can. I offered to go with him to report the incident.

That article about harassment at Smartville High School has made me really aware of harassment and bullying at my own school. Just the other day I saw some 10th-grade girls making fun of some younger girls. I went over and said, "Hey, that's not funny. Back off." They threw me a nasty look but they left her alone.

I teach English at Smartville High School. That article got me thinking about what I can do to address the issue of harassment and bullying with my students. I think our next writing assignment will be an essay about harassment and what we as a school can do about the issue.

That harassment incident made me so mad! I don't want to go to a school where that kind of thing happens. I'm going to write a series of articles about harassment and bullying for the school newspaper.

Those guys who got suspended are my friends. They told me what they were planning on doing. I told them it sounded pretty mean to me and that they would get in trouble. They just laughed. I said, "Come on. Think about how that kid's going to feel."

I saw that kid who got "canned" at lunch yesterday. I went over to talk to him because I wanted him to know that we aren't all like those 11th graders at this school. I want my school to be a welcoming place, not a place where people have to be scared.

Responding to Bullying and Harassment

CASEL SEL Competencies

SA\ Self-Awareness
DM Responsible Decision-Making

■ Agenda

Gathering: Journal and Pair Share

Agenda Review

Activity 1: Responding to Harassment and Bullying

Activity 2: Guidelines for Confronting Harassment and Bullying—Sentence Starter Brainstorm

Activity 3: Assertive Responses Triads

Debriefing

Closing: Courage Web

■ Materials

Student journals or paper for journal writing

Chart of roles used in the previous lesson: Roles in Harassment and Bullying

If desired, chart paper for listing Responses in Activity 1. This chart may also be used in the next lesson, 10-5, Interrupting Prejudice and Verbal Abuse

Handout—Confronting Harassment and Bullying: Guidelines for Targets.

Handout—Confronting Harassment and Bullying: Guidelines for Allies

Handout—Harassment and Bullying Situations to Confront

Gathering: Journal and Pair Share

1. Ask students to write for 3 or 4 minutes about why it is difficult to confront harassment and bullying.

2. Group students into pairs (see the Teaching and Learning Strategies Appendix for suggestions on random pairing). Give pairs 3 minutes to discuss their responses to the question, signaling when half of the time is up.

3. Ask for volunteers to share any new ideas that arose as a result of their discussion.

Agenda Review

Explain that now that the class has defined issues and the roles that people take in harassment and bullying situations, this lesson is an opportunity to explore what actions might be appropriate to take. There is no one, perfect way to respond to any harassment or bullying; everyone needs to have a number of choices at their disposal. The first activity will help us look at different kinds of responses, the second to brainstorm some effective responses, and the third to put some into practice with some work in groups. We'll Debrief by summarizing the experience, and in the Closing we'll generate some things that can increase the courage that facing harassment and bullying needs.

Activity 1: Responding to Harassment and Bullying

1. Refer to the chart of roles used in the previous lesson: Roles in Harassment and Bullying

   ⊙ **Target:** This is the person or group that is being harassed.

   ⊙ **Aggressor:** Also known as a bully, this person actively and repeatedly engages in behavior meant to taunt, threaten, humiliate, victimize, or physically harm the target.

   ⊙ **Instigator:** He/she spreads rumors or gossip, or makes up things to get the target in trouble. The instigator may use taunts or rumors to try to make the aggressor mad enough to harass the target. Instigating can be done verbally, using slams, the Internet, chat rooms, or graffiti in public places such as bathrooms, etc. Not all bullying and harassment has an instigator. Sometimes the aggressor is responsible for these actions.

◼ Prep

Place the Agenda on the board or on a chart

Make copies of the handout Confronting Harassment and Bullying: Guidelines for Targets—one for each student

Make copies of the handout Confronting Harassment and Bullying: Guidelines for Allies—one for each student

Make copies of the handout Harassment and Bullying Situations to Confront—one per triad

⊚ **Bystander:** A person who stands by, witnesses, or knows that the target is being harassed and does or says nothing. Sometimes bystanders think that doing nothing will prevent them from being harassed, or that it is "not their business." Bystanders can be both adults and students.

⊚ **Ally:** A person who stands up for the target by defending him/her nonviolently and by challenging the aggressor's attacks.

2. Draw three columns on the board or on chart paper. Label the columns "Avoidance," "Aggression," and "Assertion." Explain that these are three ways people can respond in a harassment or bullying situation.

3. Start with "avoidance." Ask the class what it would look like if someone was avoiding a harassment situation. What would the person be doing? How would he/she be acting? Student answers might include walking away, not saying anything, not making eye contact, etc. Record answers in the "avoidance" column. Add the definition of avoidance to the column. Avoidance means staying quiet or ignoring harassment.

4. Repeat the same process for "aggression" and "assertion." Student responses for the aggression column might include fighting, yelling, pushing, etc. Aggression means attacking back in a harassment or bullying situation. It might be more difficult for students to come up with ideas for the assertion column. Assertion means confronting the aggressor or instigator in a strong, respectful, and non-confrontational way. Student responses could include talking in a calm voice, telling your feelings, getting help, etc.

Activity 2: Guidelines for Confronting Harassment and Bullying—Sentence Starter Brainstorm

1. Distribute the handout Confronting Harassment and Bullying: Guidelines for Targets. This handout describes ways targets can assertively confront aggressors or instigators in a harassment or bullying situation. Read through the handout, inviting different students to read each point.

2. When the handout says, "OTHER THINGS THE TARGET COULD SAY …" have the group brainstorm additional assertive statements the target could make. Record ideas on chart paper and encourage students to write the ideas on their handouts as well.

3. Distribute the handout Confronting Harassment and Bullying: Guidelines for Allies. Follow the same procedure with students reading each point out loud and then brainstorming "OTHER THINGS ALLIES COULD SAY …" Record ideas on chart paper and encourage students to write the ideas on their handouts as well.

Activity 3: Assertive Responses Triads

1. Randomly divide the class into small groups of three (triads). Give each triad a copy of the handout Harassment and Bullying Situations. This handout lists nine statements which could be made by an aggressor or instigator in different types of harassment or bullying situations. Each triad should choose three of these statements they will practice confronting in the exercise. Group members should decide which role each will play in the first round:

    - **Aggressor/Feedbacker:** This person will read one of the harassment statements the group chose. After the other two triad members respond, this person will give feedback by saying, "I liked the way you …" The feedbacker should remark on what the other two said and on their body language.

    - **Target:** This person can look at the "Guidelines for Targets" handout for possible responses to the aggressor. He/she should respond to the aggressor in a firm way, using assertive body language.

    - **Ally:** This person can look at the "Guidelines for Allies" handout for possible responses to the aggressor. He/she should respond to the aggressor in a firm way, using assertive body language.

2. Give the groups a minute to decide which statements they will use and who will take each role in the first round. Allow 3 minutes for the first round. The aggressor/feedbacker should read the harassing statement to the target. The target should give a self-confident response using assertive body language. Then the ally should give a self-confident response using assertive body language. After both have responded, the feedbacker should say what he/she liked about the way the target and ally interrupted the harassment.

3. Triad members should switch roles in the second and third rounds so that everyone gets to play each role. Continue the same procedure for each round.

Debriefing

After the three rounds, debrief the activity with the following questions:

- How did it feel to be the aggressor? How did it feel when the target and ally confronted you?
- How did it feel to be the target?
- How did it feel to be the ally?
- What was difficult about responding to the harassment and bullying in the scenarios?
- What made it easier?

[Note: If students comment that some of the suggestions wouldn't work for them, acknowledge that everyone needs to feel comfortable with the choices they make in dealing with this difficult issue. However, with practice, more choices can become easier to use. Certainly if the environment values dealing with bullying and harassment, and refuses to ignore them, more people will feel comfortable in speaking up.]

> *"Men are only as respectable as they respect."*
>
> —Ralph Waldo Emeraon

Closing: Courage Web

1. Write the word COURAGE on the board or on chart paper. Explain that it takes courage to confront bullying and harassment.

2. Brainstorm courageous words or phrases targets and allies could remember that might help them be brave and take action. Write the words branched off from COURAGE. Words or phrases could include be brave, take action, you're not alone, don't be afraid, be a hero, people will respect you, etc.

Confronting Harassment and Bullying: Guidelines for Targets

1. Ignoring the problem sometimes works, but more often harassment and bullying continue (and might get worse) unless people act positively to stop it.

2. Many targets of harassment and bullying laugh in the beginning because they are nervous or embarrassed or hope that they can "laugh it off." Often the person doing the harassing and bullying and the bystanders misinterpret the laughter, thinking it means that the target doesn't mind.

3. Using insults or threats escalates the problem rather than solving it, and can get *you* in trouble instead of the person who started it. In responding, sound strong, confident, and assertive because you have the right not to be harassed. Tell the aggressor firmly,

    ◉ "I don't like it when you _____."

    ◉ "That looked and felt like harassment to me. Don't do that again."

    ◉ "Don't go there. That crosses the line."

    ◉ "What you just said felt really uncomfortable. I don't want you to say that again."

OTHER THINGS TARGETS COULD SAY …

Often, the harasser is angry about something (though being angry does not justify harassment) that has nothing to do with the target. It can help to ask calmly,

> ◉ "What's up? What are you angry about?"
>
> ◉ "Why are you doing that"?

OTHER THINGS TARGETS COULD SAY OR DO …

1. Find friends who can support you (without using threats or violence) when you confront the aggressor. This does *not* mean finding someone bigger to intimidate the harasser.

2. Exit the situation. Waiting for an apology or change of attitude risks escalating the situation. You said what you needed to say so leave the scene, turn around, walk away or focus your attention elsewhere.

Interrupting Prejudice and Verbal Abuse

CASEL SEL Competencies

SM Self-Management
SO Social Awareness

■ Agenda

Gathering: Pair Share—A Time You Experienced Prejudice

Agenda Review

Activity: "I'm Both Arab and American" by Rana Sino

Debriefing

Closing: New Insights

■ Materials

Chart from the previous lesson defining Avoidance, Aggression, and Assertion

Handout—"I'm Both Arab and American"

Handout— Six Ways to Interrupt Prejudice and Verbal Abuse

■ Prep

Place the Agenda on the board or on a chart

If desired, make copies of the story for the Activity, in order for students to read aloud

Make copies of the handout Six Ways to Interrupt Prejudice and Verbal Abuse—one per student

Gathering: Pair Share—A Time You Experienced Prejudice

1. Group students into pairs (see the Teaching and Learning Strategies Appendix for suggestions on random pairing).

2. Explain that you will pose a question, and then allow 1 minute for one partner to speak, while the other partner listens. You will then call time, the second person will respond for 1 minute while the first listens. You will then pose the second question, and then the third.

    Questions:
    ◉ Today we'll be talking about prejudice, which is generally defined as a preconceived notion or feeling formed beforehand or without knowledge, thought, or reason. Think for a moment about when you first experienced prejudice. It may have been your noticing someone else being treated in a certain way, or it may be that you have experienced prejudice. Tell your partner about that. What happened? Who was involved? Why do you think the people involved acted as they did?

    ◉ Have you ever blamed a group of people or felt anger toward them because of what a few members of that group did? What happened? Who was involved?

    ◉ Has there ever been a time when you were attacked or blamed because of the actions of a group you belonged to? (For example, as a teen, you may have heard people putting down all teenagers. Or you may have heard people putting down your racial or ethnic group.)

3. Bring the group back together, and ask for volunteers to share something they may have told their partner.

Agenda Review

Explain that prejudice surrounds us every day, and one of the most difficult things to do is to speak up against it. In the first activity, we'll be reading a story called, "I'm Both Arab and American" by Rana Sino. Then, we'll be looking at different ways to speak out and "interrupt" prejudicial statements. Explain that just as the last lesson gave us a chance to confront bullying and harassment, we'll now look at perhaps the more delicate issue of prejudice. This issue requires carefully chosen words in order to be effective without hurting the other person. Sometimes, prejudicial statements are made by people who hold opinions that they've never really examined; perhaps they've had them since childhood. Speaking up allows the other person to hear another experience, and can sometimes lead to change in values, if handled delicately and with forethought. The Activity will allow us time to think about how to do that.

The Debriefing will offer an opportunity to look at using some assertive strategies to interrupt prejudice, and the Closing will ask how we might use this in our personal lives.

Activity: "I'm Both Arab and American"

1. Read aloud "I'm Both Arab and American" by Rana Sino (from *The Courage to Be Yourself: True Stories by Teens About Cliques, Conflicts, and Overcoming Peer Pressure*) or ask for volunteers to read several paragraphs.

2. Ask the class to volunteer their ideas about why it is difficult to interrupt prejudice or verbal abuse. (For example, racist or prejudiced "jokes" and offhand remarks may be hard to interrupt because the moment passes quickly and you may not want to make a big deal out of it.) Reassure the class that interrupting these kinds of remarks is not easy—it takes courage and a skillful use of words.

3. Point out the three possible responses by using the chart from the last lesson:
   - **Avoidance:** Clamming up or ignoring it.
   - **Aggression:** Attacking back.
   - **Assertion:** Confronting in a clear and open way.

   Explain that Assertion is a healthy expression of emotion, and is an effective way to nonviolently interrupt prejudice and verbal abuse. People can respond with Assertion to stick up for themselves or to be an ally to someone else. An ally acts by standing up to help someone in a nonviolent and nonconfrontational way. Standing up to acts of prejudice, discrimination, and verbal abuse is difficult, yet necessary in order to create an environment where everyone can feel safe.

4. Distribute the handout Six Ways to Interrupt Prejudice and Verbal Abuse, and read through the information with the class.

5. Explain, When you interrupt prejudice or verbal abuse, remember to:
   - Maintain a calm, controlled tone of voice and a positive tone.
   - Use strategies from the handout, such as active listening, clarifying questions, and "I-Messages" to keep the other person's defensiveness to a minimum.
   - Use anger reducers to calm down so you can think about the words you want to say (you will not be listened to if you make the other person feel guilty or wrong). Anger reducers are anything you do to help yourself calm down, including breathing slowly, counting to ten, taking a walk, using I-Messages to own your feelings, and removing yourself from the situation.

"Prejudice is a burden that confuses the past, threatens the future and renders the present inaccessible."

—MAYA ANGELOU

Debriefing

Conduct a large group discussion:

- ◉ Looking back to Rana's story, let's use the discussion we've had, and the handout we reviewed, to come up with some other ways she could have reacted. (For example, Rana could have said, "I feel upset when I hear generalizations made about any group of people. I would appreciate it if you kept them to yourself.") Discuss any other parts of the story in which Rana could have interrupted the statements she'd heard.

- ◉ Could someone have served as her ally, or as another Arab American's ally? What might they have said?

Closing: New Insights

In a popcorn discussion style, ask:

- ◉ What new thoughts or insights emerged from this experience today?
- ◉ How might you use this experience in your daily life?

"I'm Both Arab and American"
by Rana Sino

Right after the September 11 attacks on the World Trade Center, my school decided to allow students to express their feelings about the tragedy. I understood that everyone was very upset about what had happened. I was upset too. But the teachers really should have had some consideration and asked if there were any Arab Americans amongst us who would rather leave the classroom than listen to the insults that followed.

Little did anyone know that the quiet student who was sitting by herself in the corner of the room happened to be an Arab and was listening to all of their insults, hatred, and anger. See, there was no way they could guess that I'm Arab, because I dress very American, I have light skin and blonde hair, not to mention that I talk with a New York accent.

For the first few minutes, the students were just screaming and cursing about how the United States should "bomb every one of those $%&+^." Then some students said that every Arab should die and called them smelly, dirty, and so on and so forth.

… As the students were raving on, all my teacher did was tell them to keep their voices down and watch their language.

I sat quietly … but inside I felt a flame of anger that kept growing with every disgusting word that those kids were saying. Still, I felt so bad about what had happened that I just told myself that everybody had the right to be angry.

I stayed quiet until one kid said that he had never thought about joining the army, but now he couldn't wait to enlist, get a gun, and blow the heads off of every person he sees who even looks Arab.

That's when I lost my tolerance, and screamed, "Why wait for your diploma? Why don't you just shoot me now?"

Everyone suddenly quieted down and looked at me as if something was growing out of my head. I was glad I screamed. I couldn't take hearing that hatred anymore.

I have many Arab American friends and they all feel the same way … most of them feel worse. They have been harassed because they look more Middle Eastern than I do. My friends and I have gotten abuse even from people we know. Some people from my neighborhood have called my brother and me "Bin Laden and his sister," or "terrorist twins," or "ugly A-rabs." …

The thing that really gets me is that even though I was born in Saudi Arabia, I have spent almost my whole life here and I love the United States, maybe more than a lot of people who were born here and don't understand how lucky they are to have the freedoms and comforts we do.

One reason I don't want to leave is because in this country I have learned to be an independent woman. In too many Middle Eastern countries, women have to stay home, take care of the children, and cook and clean. My father thinks in this very traditional manner … that girls and women should look up to, honor, and respect their fathers and husbands, sort of like gods.

That attitude drove me crazy when I was living with him and was one of the reasons I went into foster care. But at least in this country, I know that I am much more than a piece of property. I am allowed to go to school, get

a good job, have as many or as few children as I want, and even make more money than my husband! And I get to pick that husband too (that is, if I want one) without having to worry about my father choosing a husband for me....

Then there are the smaller things I love, such as the music and going to rock concerts.... I love the way the buildings look, and especially the fact that I would never have met my dear boyfriend, who is Hispanic American, if I had stayed....

Most important, I love that I have the freedom to say no to things I don't want to do, or say, or take, or anything!

I love this country for all those reasons and more, so when people attack me for being one of "them," they don't know a thing about how I feel. And they don't' know what it means to be an Arab, either. I have always been proud to be an Arab....

I like listening to Arab tunes.... I still like to belly dance to Lebanese music (when nobody is looking) ... I like Lebanese food like grape leaves and stuffed vegetables and chickpeas and stewed beef. I feel a strong connection to Lebanon because most of my family is still there. I believe I can love America and still be proud of being an Arab.

Seeing Arabs become the target of people's anger after September 11th has hurt, but I'm still proud to be an Arab American. It's just that now, I have to be a little more careful about who knows it. I wish other people in this country would direct their anger at Osama Bin Laden and whoever else proves to be responsible for the loss of so many innocent lives. They shouldn't make victims of more innocent people.

"I'm Both Arab and American" by Rana Sino is from *The Courage to Be Yourself: True Stories by Teens About Cliques, Conflicts, and Overcoming Peer Pressure*, used with permission from Free Spirit Publishing

Six Ways to Interrupt Prejudice and Verbal Abuse

1. Use I-Messages

   Sample starters:
   - "I don't feel comfortable when you say that."
   - "If you had said that to me, I would feel …"
   - "I don't like it when …"
   - "I wouldn't want someone to say/do that to me. I don't think anyone deserves to be treated like that."

2. Provide Accurate Information

   Sample starters:
   - "Here's what I think I know about the situation …"
   - "I don't think _____ really behaves that way."

3. Ask Clarifying Questions

   Sample starters:
   - "Can you tell me why you think that about _____?"
   - "What exactly do you mean by that?"
   - "Why does this upset you so much?"

4. Rephrase and Reflect

   Sample starters:
   - "This is what I heard you say: ___. Is that the way you meant it?" (If the discriminator uses a slur, don't repeat it. Use a letter to note the word or say "a mean word"; this way you're making it especially clear how derogatory and hurtful you find the remark to be.)

5. Share Your Perspective

   Sample starter:
   - "That sounds like an assumption to me. I don't think I know _____ well enough to say that."

6. Say What You Need

   Sample Starters:
   - "Even though I'm not _____, it hurts me to hear that word. Please don't use it again."
   - "When I'm around, I'd rather you didn't use words like that. Can you handle that?"

Becoming an Ally

CASEL SEL Competencies

SO   Social Awareness
SM   Self-Management

■ Agenda

Gathering: Journal and Pair Share

Agenda Review

Activity 1: Role Play Preparation

Activity 2: Role Play Presentation

Debriefing

Closing: Pledge

■ Materials

Handout—Responding to Bullying and Harassment: Guidelines for Targets

Handout—Responding to Bullying and Harassment: Guidelines for Allies

■ Prep

Place the Agenda on the board or on a chart

Make copies of the handout Responding to Bullying and Harassment: Guidelines for Targets —one per student

Make copies of the handout Responding to Bullying and Harassment: Guidelines for Allies —one per student

If desired, chart the role-play guidelines and/or the goals of the role plays outlined in Activity 1, #3.

Gathering: Journal and Pair Share

1. Write the quote by Edmund Burke on the board, or on chart paper, "All that is necessary for the triumph of evil is that good men do nothing." Ask students to write for 3 or 4 minutes about what they think the quote means.

2. Group students into pairs (see the Teaching and Learning Strategies Appendix for suggestions on random pairing). Give pairs 3 minutes to discuss their responses to the quote, signaling when half of the time is up.

3. Bring the class back together and ask for volunteers to say what they thought the quote meant.

Agenda Review

We have talked a great deal about the issues of harassment and bullying, what we can do to deal with these issues, and how to stand up against unfair treatment of ourselves and others. Today we're going to prepare and present some role plays in which we put our skills to the test.

Explain that the class will be preparing role plays in Activity 1, using both a handout and their own creative ideas of how to be an effective ally. During the presentation of the role plays, the class will be identifying what strategies were used, and exploring their effectiveness.

The Debriefing is an opportunity to create an extensive list of strategies, so that they can become a part of a repertoire to use in our personal lives. The Closing will provide a time for commitment in becoming an Ally for others.

Activity 1: Role Play Preparation

1. Distribute the handouts—Responding to Bullying and Harassment: Guidelines for Targets and Responding to Bullying and Harassment: Guidelines for Allies.

2. Discuss after students have read silently, or ask for volunteers to read sections. Ask for any comments. (Note: If students comment that some of the suggestions wouldn't work for them, acknowledge that everyone needs to feel comfortable with the choices they make in dealing with this difficult issue. However, with practice, more choices can become easier to use. Certainly if the environment values dealing with bullying and harassment, and refuses to ignore them, more people will feel comfortable in speaking up.)

3. Divide the class into six groups (see the Teaching and Learning Strategies Appendix for suggestions on random grouping, or if you randomly paired for the Gathering, combine two pairs into a group) and give each small group one of the role play scenarios. In each scenario, the incident is reaching a crisis point where there will be a confrontation between the characters.

4. Each group should create a brief role play (3 minutes or less) that demonstrates what could happen in this confrontation if the ally helps the target and if the bystander has a change of heart and becomes an ally. The point of the role play is to show ways that allies and bystanders can stop harassment or bullying or ways that targets can stand up for themselves. In their role plays, groups should:

   ⊙ Briefly show what happens during the incident. This should be brief because the emphasis of the role play is on how to help the target, not on the harassment or bullying.

   ⊙ Show the target trying to confront the aggressor or the instigator.

   ⊙ Show the bystander watching the incident.

   ⊙ Show the ally helping in some way.

   ⊙ Show the bystander having a change of heart and starting to help.

Role Play Guidelines

   ⊙ You can name the characters and add other details, as long as they do not detract from the main message of how to end the harassment or bullying. Names may not be people you know.

   ⊙ Do not use bad language or any real physical violence.

   ⊙ Emphasize how to be a good ally in the role play. Do not emphasize the harassment or bullying. It might be more fun to role play that part, but it is more important that you demonstrate how to be a good ally.

   ⊙ The role play will be stopped if the guidelines are not followed.

[**Cautionary Note:** Teachers or other adults should monitor the groups closely to make sure that students who are targets of harassment or bullying in real life are not forced to be targets in the role play. Teachers can assign the roles in each group if this is happening or is in danger of happening.]

Activity 2: Role Play Presentation

1. Give each group 3 minutes to present their role play to the large group. After each group's presentation, one of the group members should ask the large group these questions:

   ⊙ What type of harassment or bullying did you see in our role play?

   ⊙ What ally strategies did we demonstrate?

2. After all six groups have presented their role plays, briefly summarize the ally strategies demonstrated.

"Accept no one's definition of your life; define yourself."

—Harvey Fierstein

Debriefing

Ask:

- What did it feel like to act as an ally in the role plays?
- What did it feel like to be the target?
- How did it feel to have a change of heart as the bystander?

If groups have come up with additional effective comments, add them to the handout.

Closing: Pledge

Days after the shooting at Columbine High School in Littleton, Colorado, a group of Nashville, Tennessee students created a pledge in order to take a stand against bullying and harassment. They invited other students to sign the following pledge:

As part of my community and my school, I WILL:

- Pledge to be a part of the solution.
- Eliminate taunting from my own behavior.
- Encourage others to do the same.
- Do my part to make my community a safe place by being more sensitive to others.
- Set the example of a caring individual.
- Eliminate profanity toward others from my language.
- Not let my words or actions hurt others…
- And if others won't become a part of the solution, I WILL.

In a go-round, ask students to make one statement as a pledge.

Responding to Bullying and Harassment: Guidelines for Targets

Ignoring isolated incidents may work, but a consistent problem of harassment will probably continue unless you act to stop it.

You might try to respond in the following ways:

1. Say the aggressor's name and show respect. Sometimes this means saying something like, "Steven, I don't mean any disrespect. I just want you to know...."

2. Tell the aggressor what you don't like, and what behavior is bothering you, using any of these suggested responses or rewording a response that feels right for you.
   - "I don't like it when you _____."
   - "It doesn't feel respectful when you _____."
   - "That looked and felt like harassment to me. Don't do that again."
   - "Don't go there. That crosses the line."
   - "What you just said felt really uncomfortable. I don't want you to say that to me again."
   - "You know, I would never say that to anyone. No one needs to hear that kind of stuff here at school."
   - "Look _____, you're my friend. And I've told you before, I don't like it when you say/do _____. It feels like you don't respect my feelings. Please stop using those words. Can you do that?"
   - "I feel disrespected/upset/uncomfortable when I hear you say that to me. I don't deserve hearing that and neither does anyone else."
   - "You know, earlier today, when you said _____, I really felt uncomfortable/disrespected. Please don't say that again."

3. Exit. You don't want to wait for a response or a miraculous conversion. Waiting for an apology or change of attitude risks escalating the situation. Leaving the scene, turning around, walking the other way, or focusing attention elsewhere is what you need to do.

If you're nervous about nonviolently confronting a person who is an aggressor or an instigator, that's a good indication that it's time to inform adults about the problem. "Exiting" can sometimes be a good option.

HANDOUT

Responding to Bullying and Harassment: Guidelines for Allies

Many targets of harassment laugh at the beginning because they are nervous or embarrassed. They may believe or hope that they can just "laugh it off." Often aggressors and bystanders misinterpret the laughter, thinking it means the target doesn't mind.

Without allies, the cycle of harassment and bullying continues unchecked.

If you see someone being targeted, you might try responding in the following ways:

1. Say the aggressor's name and show respect.

2. Tell the aggressor to stop, name what you see, and why you don't like it:
   - "Knock it off with the abusive language, okay? No one deserves to hear that."
   - "I saw that and it looks like harassment to me. Lay off."
   - "If you had said that to me, I would have felt really uncomfortable/ disrespected. I don't want to hear that kind of stuff when I'm around."
   - "You know, if Mr. _____ had heard that he would have labeled that remark as harassment. Clean up the language, OK?"
   - "That really sounds like a stereotype to me. I don't know _____ well enough to make that judgment."
   - "Where did that come from? We don't say stuff like that here. That's not what this school is about. Please don't say that here."
   - "I heard that. At this school, that's not OK to say to her/him, me, or anyone else."
   - "Hey, that's an ouch. I wouldn't want anyone to say that to me."
   - "Watch the language, huh? That's not OK to say to anyone."
   - "Look _____, you're my friend. And I've told you before, I don't like it when you say/do _____ around me. It feels like you don't respect my feelings. Please stop using those words. Can you do that?"
   - "You know, earlier today, I heard you say _____ to _____. If you had said that to me I would have really felt _____. Please don't say that to her/him or anyone else."

3. Take action:
   - Help the targeted person to leave the scene.
   - Go with the targeted person to report the incident.
   - Report the incident yourself.

Role Play 1: Interrupting Sexual Harassment

Background: The target and Jean are study partners. They often hang out together after school to finish their homework. The aggressor and the instigator both secretly like Jean, but have not told her. The instigator frequently tells the aggressor that he's heard that the target and Jean are messing around. This makes the aggressor really mad. Tuesday afternoon on the bus the whole situation comes to a boil.

Target: When the aggressor and the instigator have confronted you in the past, you've tried to defend yourself with the truth. Instead of getting into an argument, you have tried being assertive and then walking away. It is really getting bad. The aggressor has started bumping you in the hall. You and he share a gym period, and all the coach says when he hears you or sees the aggressor making fun of you is, "You guys! Knock it off." You are starting to feel helpless and begin to think it would be easier just to tell Jean she needs another study partner.

Instigator: You saw Jean and the target talking after school and frequently tell the aggressor that they must be messing around. You know the aggressor secretly likes Jean, and you just like to see him get mad. You especially like to get the aggressor going when he is with his friends. You think it's hilarious when the aggressor picks on the target, especially since you like Jean too and are jealous.

Bystander: You know the instigator is lying to the aggressor, and that the instigator just likes to stir up trouble. You know from your sister, Jean's friend, that the target and Jean are just friends—in fact, the target is just a study buddy. You would like to say something, but up to this point you have felt that it's not your business.

Aggressor: Secretly, you actually like Jean but don't have the courage to ask her out. The instigator keeps telling you things about the target and Jean to the point that now every time you see the target you get really angry. You bump into him in the hall or gym class. On the bus, you call him names. You are getting angrier and angrier with each passing day.

Ally: When the instigator and the aggressor start picking on the target, you tell them, "Hey, leave him alone. He told you nothing is going on." The aggressor and instigator tell you to mind your own business, saying, "You must like the target."

Role Play 2: Interrupting Class-Related Harassment

Background: One day at lunch, the target sat down at the same table as the aggressor and his friends. When they told her to move, she said, "Why? I don't have to." The aggressor is furious and starts a campaign, fueled by the instigator, to make the target pay for acting out of line. The situation escalates until Monday morning in the hallway it explodes.

Target: You do not know why these people are picking on you. One of them seems to have made it her personal mission to make your life miserable. The aggressor and his friends are spreading rumors about you and your family. You have tried asking them, "What's up? Why are you doing this?" It's getting so bad that even when you answer a question in class, they laugh and whisper to each other, throw paper at you, and act like you have some type of disease. They push themselves as far as they can up against a wall when you walk by during class changes.

Aggressor: Your family is well-off. You have a lot of things that most students do not have, and you only want to hang out with people like yourself. The target made the mistake one day of sitting with you and your friends (some of them are instigators) at your lunch table. When you asked her to move, she said, "I don't have to." It really pissed you off, especially because she comes from a family that doesn't have much money. Each time you see her, you insult her and make fun of the way she is dressed, calling her "ghetto girl," "stinky," "raggedy-dressed loser." Your friends laugh and think it's funny.

Instigator: Your parents make sure you have the latest in electronics, games, movies, and videos. You use your phone to send the aggressor messages about the target, spreading rumors about the target's home, clothes, and choice in music. You encourage the aggressor and other friends to move when you see the target, make funny faces when she answers questions in class, and stand against the wall when the target walks by to make sure she does not touch you. You encourage the aggressor to do the same.

Bystander: You see the target get picked on by the aggressor and his friends. You feel sorry for her, but if you said something, they might notice that you don't dress the best either. You would like to say something but do not know what to say that would make them stop. Besides, everyone gets picked on sometimes.

Ally: You know your friend does not dress in designer clothes. What she wears or doesn't wear is not important to you. It's who she is that makes you really like her. You have observed that the harassment is escalating. Whenever the aggressor says things like, "Here comes no-name" or "Get your poor, raggedy self out of here" you tell the aggressor, "Leave her alone; it's not what you wear, it's who you are," and suggest that you and the target move away from the bully and his friends.

Role Play 3: Interrupting Religious and Cultural Harassment

Background: The target wears a headscarf to school because her religion requires that males and females cover their heads. She is just learning English and thought that's why she was being picked on until the aggressor started knocking off her headscarf and calling her a religion freak. The situation is getting out of control because the instigator keeps spreading rumors about the target and teasing the aggressor for not fighting. The situation explodes outside of choir class just before winter break.

Target: You dress modestly for religious reasons and try really hard to blend fashions so you won't stick out. Your religion requires that males and females cover their heads; it's just the way you were brought up so it's no big deal to you. At first you thought you were getting picked on because you are learning English, now it seems that they are picking on you because you are of a different religion. When you have tried to stand up to them, correcting them with accurate information, you are told, "What a freaking religious nutcase!"

Aggressor: You are a religious person who gets mad because a group of students won't sing Christmas carols during choir class. What do they have against Christians? Why should they get away with not participating in class? And get away with dressing so funny?

Instigator: You push the bully to tease and mock the students wearing headscarves or head coverings. You spread rumors, point when you see them, laugh at them, and tease the aggressor for not fighting them.

Bystander: Since 9/11 you have noticed that the students who speak a foreign language, dress religiously, and are otherwise different are getting ridiculed. Everyone gets teased sometimes, yet this seems so unfair. Prior to this date, other students may not have talked to them, but it was not this bad. One girl in particular calls them bad names and tries to pull the girls' headscarves. You're afraid to say anything though, because she might attack you.

Ally: You, too, have noticed that things are getting out of control at school. You believe that everyone has a right to worship as they please, that this teasing is not right. You tell the instigators that spreading misinformation about the targets' religious beliefs is wrong. You have even begun doing research on the topic of other religions so that you have accurate information. You also stand up to the meanest person of the bunch, telling her she should treat others the way she wants to be treated.

HANDOUT

Role Play 4: Interrupting Ability-Level-Related Harassment

Background: The target is in the aggressor's math and gym classes. The target sometimes gets nervous in math and gives wrong answers during math team competitions and is just not very good in soccer, which is the sport they're playing in gym right now. The aggressor is very competitive and thinks that the target is holding them back in both math and gym. The situation escalates and boils over after gym class on Friday when the soccer team loses again.

Target: You have not played soccer since you were in third grade. You are not very good at it. It is your least favorite sport. You are, however, an average student. Sometimes you make mistakes when you get nervous in class during the math team competitions, but so do other people. You do not understand why the aggressor has singled you out; everyone makes mistakes. You are getting tired of the constant teasing, ridicule, and humiliation both in class and on the field, but cannot think of a way to make it stop. You try to avoid them, but cannot do so—in gym or in math class.

Aggressor: The target gets on your nerves, yelling out wrong answers during the team competitions in math class. Even worse, the coach put him/her on your team in soccer. You like winning—in class and on the field. The target seems to trip over the ball and has difficulty passing. You tease the target with names like "dufus," "stupid," and "dumbo."

Instigator: In your opinion, the target is clumsy, can't play soccer, and even tripped over the ball during an easy goal, helping the other team to win. You tell the aggressor that if they make things uncomfortable, the target might be benched and then the team can resume their winning season. You and the aggressor make funny faces in class, sigh when the target answers questions wrong, and glare at the target during practice. You have asked your friends to do the same. You even got the aggressor to trip the target in gym class during a practice session. You just want the target to go away.

Bystander: You are school-smart and athletic, doing well in both areas of your life. You play on the league soccer team after school and you have been teased before for being smart. Though you feel sorry for the target, you are not about to make yourself one by saying anything.

Ally: You do okay in both academics and sports. You have stood up for the target in gym class before, and do so each time you see the aggressor picking on him or her. You even told the instigator, "I feel upset when you put others down. Why don't you just stop it!"

Role Play 5: Interrupting Body-Size/Shape-Related Harassment

Background: The target is trying out for the spirit team at school and has a pretty good shot at getting the last slot on the team. The instigator wants the aggressor to make it on the team. That way they can keep the team "pure." The aggressor and instigator snub the target at practice and call the target names. Just before the final team tryouts, the aggressor explodes.

Target: You feel all right with yourself and think that you look and feel good, even though you are not the smallest person in the world. You know that the instigator wants his/her friend on the team and that is the reason they tease you, make fun of your jumps, and laugh when you do the splits. You are really starting to get angry, yet do not believe that violence is the answer. You have stood up to them without putting them down, tried ignoring the comments, and even just walked away. You have even told your friends what is going on and feel a little upset that they haven't stood up for you. You are starting to feel maybe it would be better if you quit. Then, at least, the instigator and aggressor might leave you alone.

Aggressor: You believe that all people who are large-bodied do not try hard and are unattractive. You tease him/her, especially at lunch, when you and your friends make fun of what the target is eating and then laugh at the target when you see him/her eating healthy, saying things like, "You can eat all the yogurt in the world. Nothing will help you!" You increase the teasing, and even play mean jokes on the target at spirit team practice because you want to sabotage the target's chance of getting on the team.

Instigator: The target is going out for the spirit team. You want your friend to make the team, and it looks like the target has a good chance of being picked for the last slot on the team. You tell the aggressor things about the target like, "You know we have to look a 'certain way' to be on the team and he/she doesn't even come close!" You snub the target at practice and warm-ups and tell the aggressor to help you get him/her off the team so that it will open up a spot for the aggressor.

Bystander: You see the target getting teased and being called such names as "fatty," "piggy," and "living large." You have laughed, yet know it is not really funny because it hurts the target's feelings. However you, too feel a little overweight and exercise to keep your weight down. The target should do the same.

Ally: You have stood up for the target, telling the aggressor to "Leave him/her alone; he/she is not bothering you"; "What business is it of yours?"; and "We don't speak to people like that in this school."

Role Play 6: Interrupting Homophobia-Related Harassment

Background: The target's mom is divorced and has a close relationship with her sisters and female friends. The aggressor and instigator have started a rumor that the target's mom is gay and so therefore the target must be gay too. They left a note saying that on the target's desk. The situation explodes after the last class of the day.

Target: Your mom is divorced and has very close relationships with her sisters and her friends. They frequently hug good-bye and hello. Your mom's sister and your mom sometimes hold hands. You were not the most popular person in the school, but prior to the rumor getting started, you had some friends. Now even they look at you funny, move when you touch their shoulder, etc. You are confused and shamed by this rumor about your being gay, but are really enraged by the things written in the note. You are tired of it, but do not know what to do to make the harassment stop.

Aggressor: You have always heard that when two people of the same sex hold hands and hug each other they are gay. You saw the target's mother hug another woman and then heard that they were in the mall holding hands. You spread rumors around school and wrote a note that said the target's mom is a lesbian. You passed it around last week in each class and then left it on the target's desk during last period on Monday.

Instigator: You are the one who told the aggressor that you saw the target's mother and another woman holding hands in the mall. You wrote some things about the aggressor and the target on the bathroom wall and helped pass the note around school.

Bystander: You do not believe the rumors that are being spread about the target and his/her mother. You believe that people have the right to live their lives as they want and think that what is being done to the target and his/her family is mean. Despite feeling this way, the last time you said something to the aggressor, you were accused of being gay, therefore, you are just staying out of it. You feel sorry for the target.

Ally: You cannot believe what you are hearing. The target's mother and your mother are friends. You stand up for the target, have spoken to a counselor about the rumors, and have confronted the instigator, aggressor, and their friends in the past, being assertive, but not mean. It is getting hard for you to keep standing up and you feel like you are the only one doing anything about it—especially when adults hear this stuff and do not say anything.

Teaching and Learning Strategies

Here are descriptions of the teaching and learning strategies used in these lessons. Feel free to adapt your own strategies to the sessions.

Brainstorming

A process for generating as many ideas as possible. The leader proposes a topic or question and lists group members' responses on the board or on chart paper. Here are a few helpful brainstorming guidelines to share with your group:

- All ideas are accepted; every idea will be written down.
- No one makes a comment, either positive or negative, on any of the ideas presented.
- Push for quantity. Say anything that comes to mind, even if it sounds silly.
- Think about what others have suggested and use those ideas to get your brain moving along new lines.

Concentric Circles

This activity gives group members a chance to share with a variety of partners. Divide the teens into two equal groups. (If you don't have two equal groups, you can join one.) One group forms a circle facing outward. The other group forms a second circle around that one, facing inward. Each person in the inner circle faces a partner in the outer circle. (If you don't have enough space to make circles, parallel rows will suffice.) Tell the group that they will each have about 45 seconds to share with their partners and that all pairs will speak simultaneously (pair members take turns). Identify whether the inside partners or the outside partners will speak first. Pose a question to the group and begin timing. When time is up, the other partners respond to the question. When both partners have answered the question, ask one of the circles to move one, two, or three spaces to the right. Then pose another question and repeat the process. To ensure group members interact with a range of partners, the circle should rotate for each question. Concentric circles is less intimate than other group sharing activities, such as microlabs and pair shares, and is more appropriate for less sensitive or difficult topics. It's also good for situations when you want teens to get multiple responses and be more active. It helps build class unity and group participation.

Go-Rounds

Gives every member of the group a chance to respond to a statement or question. This activity is especially useful for sharing feelings and experiences. In go-rounds, the group is seated in a circle (if possible). Circles greatly facilitate open communication by putting everyone on an equal footing, especially when the leader joins the group. In addition, everyone in the group can look directly at the person who is speaking. This encourages everyone to pay attention to one another and fosters a sense of community.

Introduce the topic of the go-round in the form of a statement or question. The topic can be general so that most group members will be able to comment (for example, "What was something you enjoyed about our last lesson?"), or it can be something specifically related to the content of a session. Group members take turns responding, going around the circle. People always have the right to pass when it's their turn to speak, though even those who find it difficult to speak in groups often will speak during a go-round. After everyone has responded, you can go back to those who passed to see if they now want to contribute.

Journal Writing

Teens can explore conflict through various writing activities. Several sessions ask group members to respond to questions in journals. You may want to distribute journals to the group before the first session and ask them to record their reactions to the sessions as you progress. Journal prompts urge group members to review conflicts they have experienced, examine feelings and opinions they hold, and brainstorm or discuss ideas. Journal entries do not have to be long—it is the ability to connect with feelings and experiences that counts, not the length of the entry. Assure the group their journal writing will not be graded or collected, and no one will be required to share what they have written.

In some sessions we provided a series of journal prompts. In these sessions, you will read aloud a statement or question and ask the students to write their responses in their journals. Offer the group only a *short* time to write on each question (one minute is fine; three minutes is the maximum). Tell them they must keep writing without stopping (writing nonstop frees up emotions and ideas). If they say they don't have anything to write, tell them they can keep writing "I have nothing to say" until something comes to them. When time is up, read the next prompt, again allowing a short period of time for responding.

In our experiences with teens we've found that a few minutes of freewriting deepens their reflections and often opens up topics for discussion that would not otherwise be raised by discussion alone.

Microlabs

The microlabs structure enables participants to examine their experiences in the intimacy of a small group. It is designed to maximize personal sharing and active listening. In groups of three or four, group members take turns responding to questions. Each person has an equal period of time to respond. When one person is speaking, others give the speaker their full attention and do not interrupt or ask questions. Speakers should use "I-messages" when discussing what they said, thought, and felt. When introducing microlabs, stress the importance of confidentiality. What is shared in a microlab should not be repeated outside the group.

Opinion Continuums

This technique allows group members to express their own attitudes and opinions and, most importantly, to realize that it is okay to hold a different opinion from others in the class. To begin activities using this technique, draw a line on the board or on the floor with "Strongly Agree" at one end, "Strongly Disagree" at the other, and "Unsure" in the middle. You then read a statement and group members position themselves along the line to indicate their opinions. Alternatively, you can use a person or object in the room as a symbol and ask group members to position themselves according to how they feel about the thing being symbolized. After group members have positioned themselves in the opinion continuum, you can invite them to explain their positions.

Pair Shares

This technique involves multiple, simultaneous conversations. Students share responses to a question in one of two ways: One student focuses on practicing listening skills while the other partner speaks, then partners switch roles; students engage in a dialogue with each other and agree on a response to share with the larger group. Like microlabs, pair shares are more intimate than large group-centered activities, such as concentric circles or popcorn-style sharing. When you want group members to come up with deeper, more thoughtful responses, a pair share is a good option.

Popcorn-Style Sharing

This method promotes free expression of ideas in a nonjudgmental atmosphere. A set amount of time (usually about four minutes) is allotted for the whole group to share ideas on a topic—it works best when group members sit in a circle. You may pose the topic, or invite teens to bring up a theme from the assigned reading. Popcorn-style sharing means that rather than going around the circle one by one, students voice their opinions in a random order. There is no pressure to speak up.

Rotation Stations

This technique allows teens to brainstorm responses to a series of questions in a small group. Write questions or problems on large sheets of newsprint or chart paper and post the questions in different areas around the room. Divide teens into groups of three or four and ask each smaller group to stand at one of the stations. Give them two minutes to brainstorm two or three responses to the question or problem. Have them write their responses on the newsprint or chart paper, then ask each group to move to the next station and give their responses to another question.

Webbing or Concept Maps

Choose a key word or concept from the session story and write it in the center of the board or flip chart. Ask the group to suggest words and ideas they associate with that word or concept. Add the new words and ideas to the board with a line stemming out from the word in the center. To visually connect various aspects of the key concept and the following associations, you can cluster related ideas together.

Random Grouping

Research tells us that no matter how hard we try to be fair, we can't help making biased choices. Using random strategies for grouping students creates opportunities for students to get to know and work with all of their classmates. Using these strategies also gets you off the hook of being the one responsible for "making" a particular student work with someone not of his/her choosing.

◎ *Pairing*

There are several strategies that may be used. Having cards with a different student's name on each one, shuffling, and then taking whichever card is on top is one way. Another way is to use pairs of cards (postcards, etc.) that are shuffled and distributed. Students find the person with the matching card to form a pair.

◎ *Forming Small Groups*

Forming small, cooperative working groups randomly can be both fun and effective.

Have students count off. To make nine groups of three in a class of twenty-seven, have students count off from one to nine three times. Then have all the one's, two's, three's (and so on) come together as groups.

Cut postcards or pictures into pieces, or create puzzle pieces using index cards. Distribute the pieces, and ask students to move around the room looking for others whose pieces complete the picture or puzzle.

Playing cards are useful for making groups of four. For example, if you have twenty-four students, you would separate the suits and six cards with the same face value. You would then have all students with cards of the same face value come together. For groups of six you would have students holding hearts, spades, diamonds, or clubs come together.

Other options for grouping may connect to a topic you're studying in your academic curriculum. For example, creating index cards using "healthy snacks" or food within a food group can reinforce a health or science lesson on nutrition and healthy eating. Characters in novels the class has read can come together by groups.

These Teaching and Learning Strategies have been adapted with permission from *A Leader's Guide to The Courage to Be Yourself* by Al Desetta and Sherrie Gammage with Educators for Social Responsibility (Free Spirit Publishing, 2006)

Guidelines for Role Plays

What is Role Playing?

Role playing is temporarily taking on a role and acting out a situation for the purpose of learning new skills or exploring new ways of relating to others.

In conflict resolution, role playing lets students practice and experiment with new skills and behaviors to see how they feel, how the behavior "works," and what problems come up. It gives you, the teacher, the opportunity to give feedback and assess how well the student is acquiring and using new skills and understandings.

Types of Role Plays

All of these types of role plays can be scripted ahead of time or improvised on the spot by students.

Small Groups: Three or four students per group, with students taking turns as actors and observers.

Hassle Lines: The class forms two lines facing each other. Each actor in one line role plays with the actor facing her in the opposite line. The role plays take place simultaneously. Everyone in each line plays the same role.

Demonstration: The teacher and one or two students rehearse a role play before class and perform the role play for the class.

Whole Group: The class is divided into two or more groups. Everyone in the group speaks from the perspective of one assigned role. The teacher facilitates by calling on students.

Role Play Techniques

Role Reversal: Actors switch roles halfway through the role play.

Fish Bowl: The audience forms a circle around the actors and comments on the action or motivations of the actors.

Replacements: As the actors role play, observers from the audience may tap them on the shoulder and replace them.

Role Play Rules

- Stop everything when the teacher says "Freeze!"
- No booing or hissing from the audience.
- No swearing.
- No real or pretend physical fighting.

The Teacher's Role

The teacher sets up the role play and explains the rules. The teacher also facilitates the discussion at the end of the role play. This discussion is very important, for this is where students receive feedback on their use of a particular skill.

To do this you need to:

- Teach the class how to give appropriate feedback;
- Demonstrate feedback skills;
- Praise students when they give appropriate feedback.

Try to model the following feedback behaviors. You may also need to point out to students what you are doing, so they will learn to give similar types of feedback.

- Talk about the behavior, not the person. Role plays are designed to promote behavioral skills, so it is important that feedback be directed at the behavior. For example, instead of saying: "You sounded like you wanted to solve the problem," say: "You said 'Let's work it out' and that let the other person know you wanted to solve the problem."
- Be specific. Tell students exactly what they are doing right or what could be improved. For example, instead of saying: "That was good," say: You asked the other person what he or she wanted in the situation."
- Emphasize what was done well and suggest improvements for next time. For example: "You did a good job of looking her in the eye. Speaking up a bit more might be helpful next time."
- Suggest choices rather than giving instructions. Explore the consequences of the new choices. For example, instead of saying: "ask her when she'll be finished with the tape recorder," say: "What do you think would happen if you asked her when she would be finished with the tape recorder?"

Questions for Processing the Role Play

The types of questions you ask will influence the kind of feedback you get. Ask each actor:

- How did you feel playing the role?
- What did you notice yourself doing?
- How did the other person(s) respond to your actions?
- What do you think you did well?
- What might you have done differently or better?

Ask the observers:

- How did you feel as you watched the role play?
- How did the conflict develop? How did it escalate?
- What stands out about how the actors talked/behaved?
- Why do you think they behaved as they did?
- What did they do that made the conflict better or worse?
- What might they have done differently?

For everyone:

- Have you ever been in a situation like this one?
- How did you handle it? How did it turn out?
- What might be another way to t handle this situation?

End the discussion by summarizing the major issues. Tie these issues to the purpose of the role play.

Facilitating Role Plays

1. Explain the purpose of the role play, such as practicing problem solving, trying new ways of communicating in conflicts, or practicing mediation. To learn from the role play, students need to know why they are doing it.

2. Describe the role play situation and the characters, as well as the type of role play it will be.

3. Review the role play rules.

4. Assign roles to players, taking care not to choose someone who might over-identify with the part. Give the roles fictional names.

5. Brief the actors; make sure they understand what the conflict is.

6. Brief the audience. As observers, what should they look/listen for?

7. Start the action. Intervene or coach only if absolutely necessary.

8. If the role play doesn't come to a natural end, cut it off gently.

9. Thank the role players, using their real names.

Once students are experienced with simple role plays, they can begin to develop their own role plays:

1. Have the class brainstorm situations.

2. Choose one situation and flesh out the underlying problem or issues involved.

3. Develop the specific roles: their ages, gender, names, characteristics. How do the characters feel about each other? The situation?

4. Develop the background: What events led up to the current situation?

5. Decide on any supporting or secondary characters and develop them, defining their roles in the situation.

6. Choose a beginning point for the role play.

These Guidelines for Role Plays have been adapted from ESR's *Conflict Resolution in the High School* by Carol Miller Lieber (Educators for Social Responsibility, 1998)

Cyber-bullying

Cyber-bullying can be defined as "willful and repeated harm inflicted through the use of computers, cell phones, and other electronic devices.[1]"

Cyber-bullying can take many forms. Nancy Willard, in *Cyberbullying and Cyberthreats: Responding to the Challenge of Online Social Aggression, Threats, and Distress*, defines six forms that are the most common:

- **Harassment:** Repeatedly sending offensive, rude, and insulting messages.
- **Denigration:** Distributing information about another that is derogatory and untrue through posting it on a Web page, sending it to others through email or instant messaging, or posting or sending digitally altered photos of someone .
- **Flaming:** Online "fighting" using electronic messages with angry, vulgar language.
- **Impersonation:** Breaking into an email or social networking account and using that person's online identity to send or post vicious or embarrassing material to/about others.
- **Outing and Trickery:** Sharing someone's secrets or embarrassing information, or tricking someone into revealing secrets or embarrassing information and forwarding it to others.
- **Cyber Stalking:** Repeatedly sending messages that include threats of harm or are highly intimidating, or engaging in other online activities that make a person afraid for his or her safety (depending on the content of the message, it may be illegal).

Outcomes of Cyber-bullying

At the White House Conference on Bullying Prevention in 2011, Drs. Hinduja and Patchin presented a compelling overview of cyber-bullying. They reported that research confirms many detrimental outcomes associated with cyber-bullying. First, many targets of cyber-bullying report feeling depressed, sad, angry, and frustrated[2], and these emotions have been correlated with delinquency and interpersonal violence among youth[3].

While often similar in terms of targeting peers with hurtful words or threats, bullying and cyber-bullying have many differences that can make the latter even more devastating, explain Drs. Hinduja and Patchin. First, victims sometimes do not know who the bully is, or why they are being targeted. The cyber-bully can cloak his or her identity behind a computer or cell phone using anonymous email addresses or pseudonymous screen names[4]. Second, the hurtful actions of a cyber-bully are viral; that is, a large number of people can be involved in a cyber-attack on a victim, or at least find out about the incident with a few keystrokes or clicks of the mouse. The perception, then, is that absolutely everyone is in on the joke.

APPENDIX 3

Third, it is often easier to be cruel using technology because cyber-bullying can be done from a physically distant location, and the bully doesn't have to see the immediate response of the target[5]. In fact, some teens simply might not recognize the serious harm they are causing because they are sheltered from the victim's response. Finally, while parents and teachers are doing a better job supervising youth at school and at home, many adults don't have the technological know-how to keep track of what teens are up to online. As a result, a victim's experience may be missed and a bully's actions may be left unchecked. Even if bullies are identified, many adults find themselves unprepared to adequately respond.

A Growing Problem

Cyber-bullying is a growing problem because increasing numbers of teens are using and have completely embraced interactions via computers and cell phones. Two-thirds of youth go online every day for schoolwork, to keep in touch with their friends, to play games, to learn about celebrities, to share their digital creations, or for many other reasons[6]. Because the online communication tools have become an important part of their lives, it is not surprising that some teens have decided to use these devices to be malicious or menacing toward others. The fact that teens are connected to technology 24/7 means they are susceptible to victimization around the clock[7]. Apart from a measure of anonymity, it is also easier to be hateful using typed words rather than words spoken face-to-face. And because some adults have been slow to respond to cyber-bullying, many cyber-bullies feel that there are little to no consequences for their actions.

Cyber-bullying Prevention

The most important preventive step is to educate the school community about responsible Internet interactions. Students need to know that all forms of bullying are wrong and that those who engage in harassing or threatening behaviors will be subject to discipline. It is therefore important to discuss issues related to the appropriate use of online communications technology in various areas of the general curriculum—and not just in technology-related classes. To be sure, these messages should be reinforced in classes that regularly utilize technology. Signage also should be posted in the computer lab or at each computer workstation to remind students of the rules of acceptable use. In general, it is crucial to establish and maintain a school climate of respect and integrity where violations result in informal or formal sanction[8].

Furthermore, school district personnel should review their harassment and bullying policies to see if they allow for the discipline of students who engage in cyber-bullying. If their policy covers it, cyber-bullying incidents that occur at school—or that originate off campus but ultimately result in a substantial disruption of the learning environment—are well within a school's legal authority to intervene. The school then needs to make it clear to students, parents, and all staff that these behaviors are unacceptable and will be subject to discipline.

1. Hinduja, S. & Patchin, J. W. (2009). *Bullying Beyond the Schoolyard: Preventing and Responding to Cyberbullying.* Thousand Oaks, CA: Sage Publications.

2. Hinduja, S. & Patchin, J. W. (2007). Offline consequences of online victimization: School violence and delinquency. *Journal of School Violence,* 6(3), 89-112; Hinduja, S. & Patchin, J. W. (2008). Cyberbullying: An exploratory analysis of factors related to offending and victimization. *Deviant Behavior,* 29(2), 129-156; Hinduja, S. & Patchin, J. W. (2009). *Bullying Beyond the Schoolyard: Preventing and Responding to Cyberbullying.* Thousand Oaks, CA: Sage Publications; Kowalski, R. & Limber, S. (2007). Electronic bullying among middle school students. *Journal of Adolescent Health,* 41(6), S22-S30; Li, Q. (2007). Bullying in the New Playground: A Research into Cyberbullying and Cyber Victimization. *Australasian Journal of Educational Technology,* 23(4), 435-454.

3. Berson, I. R., Berson, M. J., & Ferron, J. (2002). Emerging risks of violence in the digital age: Lessons for educators from an online study of adolescent girls in the United States. *Journal of School Violence,* 1(2), 51-72; Cowie, H. & Berdondini, L. (2002). The expression of emotion in response to bullying. *Emotional & Behavioural Difficulties,* 7(4), 204-214; Ybarra, M.L. & Mitchell, K.J. (2007). Prevalence and frequency of Internet harassment instigation: Implications for adolescent health. *Journal of Adolescent Health,* 41(2), 189-195.

4. Hinduja, S. & Patchin, J. W. (2008). Cyberbullying: An exploratory analysis of factors related to offending and victimization. *Deviant Behavior,* 29(2), 129-156;

5. Willard, Nancy E. (2007). *Cyberbullying and Cyberthreats: Responding to the Challenge of Online Social Aggression, Threats, and Distress.* Champaign, IL: Research Press.

6. Lenhart, A., Purcell, K., Smith, A., Zickuhr, K. (2010). Social media and young adults. Pew Internet Project and American Life Survey. Retrieved from http://www.pewinternet.org/Reports/2010/Social-Media-and-Young-Adults.aspx.

7. Kowalski, R. M., Limber, S. P. & Agatston, P.W. (2008). *Cyber Bullying: Bullying in the Digital Age.* Malden, MA: Wiley-Blackwell.

8. David, S. & Davis, J. (2007). *Schools Where Everyone Belongs: Practical Strategies for Reducing Bullying.* Champaign, IL: Research Press.

What Students and Teachers Need to Know about Harassment

Many schools, districts, student clubs, and states have adopted guidelines for harassment and bullying. Part of a good prevention program includes providing students with this information. This is best done in the beginning lessons, which deal with identifying bullying and harassment. Students need to know that, should harassment be proved, there are often harsh consequences for the aggressors.

On October 26, 2010, the United States Department of Education published a "Dear Colleague" letter[9] that explains educators' legal obligations to protect students from student-on-student racial and national-origin harassment, sexual and gender-based harassment, and disability harassment. In part, it states, "I am writing to remind you, however, that some student misconduct that falls under a school's anti-bullying policy also may trigger responsibilities under one or more of the federal antidiscrimination laws enforced by the Department's Office for Civil Rights (OCR). As discussed in more detail below, by limiting its response to a specific application of its anti-bullying disciplinary policy, a school may fail to properly consider whether the student misconduct also results in discriminatory harassment."

The statutes that OCR enforces include Title VI of the Civil Rights Act of 1964 (Title VI), which prohibits discrimination on the basis of race, color, or national origin; Title IX of the Education Amendments of 1972 (Title IX), which prohibits discrimination on the basis of gender; Section 504 of the Rehabilitation Act of 1973 (Section 504); and Title II of the Americans with Disabilities Act of 1990 (Title II). Section 504 and Title II prohibit discrimination on the basis of disability. School districts may violate these civil rights statutes and the Department's implementing regulations when peer harassment based on race, color, national origin, sex, or disability is sufficiently serious that it creates a hostile environment and such harassment is encouraged, tolerated, not adequately addressed, or ignored by school employees.

Is Your Classroom Ready for This Curriculum?

This curriculum emphasizes a student-centered approach that follows students' thinking and concerns in ways that build on their own knowledge and connect their own life experiences to what's happening in the larger society.

A curriculum of this type works best in a safe and caring classroom. In a safe classroom all students participate and all students feel that they belong. They know that their individual and cultural differences will be accepted and valued as much as the things that they share in common. Teachers show that everyone counts by balancing the emphasis on individual achievement with a commitment to the well-being of the whole classroom community.

In safe classrooms, students feel comfortable expressing their feelings and concerns. They know that they can make mistakes without being ridiculed, deal with their differences constructively, and disagree respectfully. The lessons in this curriculum work best in a classroom where each student can develop his or her own voice and where listening to peers matters as much as listening to teachers.

Before you begin, it is helpful to know what is occurring in the lives of the students in your classroom. Are students being bullied? Are there some who are targets and some who are perpetrators? Knowing this will help you to facilitate the lessons.

School-wide Commitment

Implementing Bullying Prevention Programs in Schools: A How-To Guide by Jones, Doces, Swearer, and Collier provides four important elements that an effective prevention program needs to have:

- ⊙ A structured curriculum that provides youth with materials over at least several sessions and includes:
  - detailed information on how to implement each lesson
  - lesson materials
  - specific text for presenters
  - procedures for training teachers or other presenters

One-shot assemblies or pulling a few bits and pieces from a program is not going to make a difference for your youth.

- ⊙ The program teaches youth new skills. These should be spelled out in the program materials. Research shows that this is critical to helping youth change their behavior. Lecture-only programs do not do this.
- ⊙ Activities must let youth practice these new skills in active ways. The programs that schools consider should include some combination of classroom discussion periods, engaging and thought-provoking activities, and role playing.
- ⊙ For bullying in particular, the program needs to take a whole-school or community approach to prevention. The best programs all offer training for school staff, involvement of parents, and assistance to help the school improve its response to bullying concerns and reports.

Bullying prevention programs will also address the specific needs of students and staff in recognizing, reporting and effectively dealing with bullying incidents. The most effective bullying prevention programs have Social and Emotional Learning components embedded in them. A very strong approach would be to implement both types of programs. Schools can think about SEL programs as a foundation upon which the bullying-specific content should be delivered.

The best SEL programs teach youth the following skills:

- ⊙ Self-regulation (controlling impulses; focusing, sustaining, and shifting attention; listening to and remembering information; empathy training)
- ⊙ Perspective-taking (appreciating similarities and differences; recognizing and identifying the feelings of others; understanding that feelings can change and are complex)
- ⊙ Emotion management (recognizing and identifying one's own feelings; learning strategies for calming down strong emotions; managing stress/anxiety)

- Problem-solving (learning a process for solving problems; goal setting)
- Communication skills (being assertive; being respectful; negotiating and compromising)
- Friendship skills (cooperation, including others, joining in with others)

Jones, Doces, Swearer, and Collier further state that the best bullying prevention programs should ideally include the above SEL skills and the following:

- Training for all school staff and parents on the "psychology" of bullying
- Training for all school staff and parents on procedures for how to effectively handle bullying reports, including the school's process for and policies around dealing with bullying reports
- Training for teachers on how to deliver the program, including some training around managing relationships and behaviors in the classroom as well as monitoring their own behaviors that are modeled for students
- Training for "Coaches"—people who will work one-on-one with both the students doing the bullying and the students being bullied
- Guidance around establishing policies and procedures, even if it's just a checklist for schools to make sure they are in compliance with district/state/federal laws
- Classroom curricula that:
  - Teach students what bullying is: how to recognize when it's happening to you or someone else
  - Clearly state and reiterate rules, processes, and consequences regarding bullying
  - Teach students assertiveness and communication skills that will help them refuse bullying, whether it is happening to themselves or someone else
  - Teach students skills and strategies for being an effective bystander: supporting the person who was bullied, not joining in, reporting, defusing the situation if possible
  - Teach students skills and the process for reporting bullying, including who to report to
  - All skills must be practiced and reinforced

- Guidance around consequences of bullying:
  - Recommendations for appropriate and graduated consequences, including restorative justice (also sometimes called reparative justice) practice options and mental health interventions, when necessary

Implementation

These lessons have been taught in a variety of settings. Classroom teachers in academic subjects have found that beginning the year with pro-social activities helps to start the year on a positive note. However, there are many other possibilities: advisory, youth leadership programs, new school orientation, freshmen seminars, health education classes, humanities classes, special workshops for students, and out-of-school time youth programs. These lessons can also become a vital part of a peer education program, the potential of which is outlined in an appendix to this curriculum.

Students need a time and a place to discuss the effects of unwanted and unwelcome comments and actions. All students deserve adults in their lives who provide good models, are a listening ear, and who work with them to address the issues.

Bullying and harassment may never totally disappear, but when we intentionally teach how to recognize instances and have ideas on how to deal with them, schools can be safer places to live and learn.

APPENDIX 5

Recommended Resources

In addition to the books, articles, and other resources referred to in these lessons, these resources offer additional perspectives on ways to counter bullying and harassment in middle and high schools.

Books

The Advisory Guide by Rachel A. Poliner and Carol Miller Lieber (Educators for Social Responsibility, 2004)

The Bully, the Bullied, and the Bystander by Barbara Coloroso (HarperCollins, 2003)

Conflict Resolution in the High School by Carol Miller Lieber (Educators for Social Responsibility, 1998)

Conflict Resolution in the Middle School by William J. Kreidler (Educators for Social Responsibility, 1997)

Connected and Respected: Lessons from The Resolving Conflict Creatively Program by Jane Harrison and Ken Breeding (Educators for Social Responsibility, 2007)

The Courage to Be Yourself: True Stories by Teens About Cliques, Conflicts, and Overcoming Peer Pressure by Al Desetta (Free Spirit Publishing, 2005)

Cyberbullying and Cyberthreats: Responding to the Challenge of Online Social Aggression, Threats, and Distress by Nancy E. Willard (Research Press, 2007)

A Leader's Guide to The Courage to Be Yourself by Al Desetta and Sherrie Gammage (Free Spirit Publishing, 2006)

Partners in Learning by Carol Miller Lieber (Educators for Social Responsibility, 2002)

Teen Cyberbullying Investigated: Where do Your Rights End and Consequences Begin by Judge Tom Jacobs (Free Spirit Publishing, 2010)

Vicious: True Stories by Teens About Bullying edited by Hope Vanderberg of Youth Communications (Free Spirit Publishing, 2012)

Online Resources

Teaching Tolerance – http://www.tolerance.org

Gay, Lesbian & Straight Education Network – http://www.glsen.org and http://www.nonamecallingweek.org

Common Sense Media – http://www.commonsensemedia.org

PACER Center – http:// www.pacer.org/bullying and http://www.pacerteensagainstbullying.org

EducationWorld – http://educationworld.com

Media Smarts – http://MediaSmarts.ca

Race Bridges for Schools – http://racebridgesforschools.com

Cyberbullying Research Center – http://cyberbullying.us

Additional Research

- Implementing Bullying Prevention Programs in Schools: A How-To Guide (Draft) April 16, 2012 by Lisa Jones, Mia Doces, Susan Swearer, and Anne Collier; part of "The Kinder & Braver World Project: Research Series," available online at http://cyber.law.harvard.edu/sites/cyber.law.harvard.edu/files/ImplementingBullyingPrevention.pdf

- The White House Conference on Bullying Prevention, 2011, available online at http://www.stopbullying.gov/resources-files/white-house-conference-2011-materials.pdf

WORKS CONSULTED

In addition to the source material cited in the Foreword and Acknowledgments and the sources cited in endnotes throughout, the following resources provided valuable material, inspiration, and information that shaped the creation of *Countering Bullying and Harassment*'s lessons:

Ken Breeding and Jane Harrison, *Connected and Respected: Lessons from The Resolving Conflict Creatively Program*, Volumes 1 and 2. Cambridge, MA: Educators for Social Responsibility, 2007.

Al Desetta, editor, *The Courage to Be Yourself: True Stories by Teens About Cliques, Conflicts, and Overcoming Peer Pressure*. Minneapolis, MN: Free Spirit Publishing, 2005.

Al Desetta and Sherrie Gammage, *A Leader's Guide to The Courage to Be Yourself*. Minneapolis, MN: Free Spirit Publishing, 2005.

Lisa Jones, Mia Doces, Susan Swearer, and Anne Collier, *Implementing Bullying Prevention Programs in Schools: A How-To Guide (DRAFT)*. The Kinder & Braver World Project: Research Series, April 16, 2012.

Linda Lantieri, Carol Miller Lieber, and Tom Roderick, *Conflict Resolution in the High School*. Cambridge, MA: Educators for Social Responsibility, 1998.

Carol Miller Lieber, *Making Learning Real: Reaching and Engaging All Learners in Secondary Classrooms*. Cambridge, MA: Educators for Social Responsibility, 2009.

Carol Miller Lieber, *Partners in Learning: From Conflict to Collaboration in Secondary Classrooms*. Cambridge, MA: Educators for Social Responsibility, 2002.

Rachel A. Poliner and Carol Miller Lieber, *The Advisory Guide*. Cambridge, MA: Educators for Social Responsibility, 2004.

Nancy E. Willard, *Cyberbullying and Cyberthreats: Responding to the Challenge of Online Social Aggression, Threats, and Distress*. Champaign, IL: Research Press, 2007.

ABOUT THE AUTHOR

Jane Harrison has more years of experience than she sometimes likes to admit, and most of those have been in the classroom. It was in the pursuit of materials to improve the learning climate of her own classroom that led her to begin to implement some of the concepts that you'll see in this curriculum. The changes that she saw in the students, in herself, and in her relationship to the students, are what led her to begin her work with Educators for Social Responsibility.

Over the last twenty years, she has worked both nationally and internationally with schools, providing training for students, school staffs and parents. Classroom mentoring has allowed Jane to work with students from pre-kindergarten through high school, in rural, suburban, and urban settings. This has provided a rich source of experiences that inform the lessons that you'll be working with in this book.

Jane hopes that *Countering Bullying and Harassment: Skill-Based Lessons to Move from Bystander to Ally* will help teachers create a respectful and caring environment where learning can thrive. She owes a great deal of gratitude to her own children, who gave her the opportunity to continually improve and refine her own conflict resolution skills, and who now provide her with constant love and support.

ABOUT
EDUCATORS FOR SOCIAL RESPONSIBILITY

Founded in 1982, ESR is a national leader in school reform and provides professional development, consultation, and educational resources to adults who teach young people in preschool through high school.

ESR creates, disseminates and teaches core practices that:

1. Reduce educational disparities and facilitate equal access to quality instruction and opportunities for students. ESR helps schools build a positive climate and culture; a disciplined and supportive learning environment; and personalized, high achieving classrooms that promote healthy development and academic success for all students.

2. Help students develop and strengthen social skills, emotional competencies, and qualities of character that increase personal and interpersonal efficacy and cultivate social responsibility. ESR helps schools build high quality social and emotional learning programs and initiatives that promote respect and help to reduce intolerance, harassment and bullying, and risky and aggressive student behaviors.

ESR has a long history and a wealth of experience facilitating the change process and much practical expertise in how to create positive learning environments in today's schools. Our work with principals, school leadership  teams, faculty, students, and families is informed by current research and the "best practices" in educational leadership, instructional reform, prevention, and youth development.

Visit our website (*www.esrnational.org*) for more information and to sign up for our free monthly e-newsletter.

We can be reached at:

Educators for Social Responsibility

23 Garden Street

Cambridge, MA 02138

617-492-1764

617-864-5164 fax

educators@esrnational.org

ESR suggests the following resources to extend the work you can do in your school to build a positive climate and culture for powerful teaching and learning:

The Courage to Be Yourself: True Stories by Teens About Cliques, Conflicts, and Overcoming Peer Pressure, edited by Al Desetta, M.A., with Educators for Social Responsibility
In *The Courage to Be Yourself*, 26 teens write about facing challenges and how difficult life can be for today's teens—especially when they're bullied, picked on, pressured, excluded, and disrespected. With searing honesty, they write about what it's like to be labeled and judged because they are different. The teens in *The Courage to Be Yourself* use conflict to become stronger, better people. They ask themselves tough questions that many teens ask, like: Why does everyone have such a problem with me? Why can't people accept me for who I am? Should I change myself to fit in?

A Leader's Guide to The Courage to Be Yourself, by Al Desetta, M.A., with Sherrie Gammage, with Educators for Social Responsibility
Provides teachers, counselors and advisory leaders an array of discussion tools and activities to use with students to explore the different stories in classroom or advisory settings.

Conflict Resolution in the High School, by Carol Miller Lieber with Linda Lantieri and Tom Roderick
Designed to help secondary educators teach essential conflict resolution skills and concepts at the high school level. The themes of the curriculum are: conflict resolution and problem solving, building community and creating a Peaceable Classroom, diversity and inter-group relations, and emotional and social development. Includes sections on how to implement the curriculum at your school, how to assess student learning, and how to infuse conflict resolution into the standard curriculum.

Conflict Resolution in the Middle School, by William J. Kreidler
Highly acclaimed, this guide features 28 skill-building sections to help students address the conflicts that come with adolescence. Recent additions to the guide include seven implementation models; sections on creating a classroom for teaching conflict resolution, developing staff and parent support, and assessing student learning; an infusion section that includes math and science; and a section on adolescent development exploring gender and race. The *Student Workbook and Journal* available to accompany *Conflict Resolution in the Middle School* allows students to track their challenges and successes as they encounter conflicts.

For more information about these and other resources available from Educators for Social Responsibility, visit our online bookstore at www. esrnational.org/store or call our order line at 800-370-2515, x 33.